Women of The Cross

With Meditations For Holy Week

Kingdom Publishers

Copyright© Frances E Wilson 2025

All rights reserved. No part of this book may be reproduced in any form by photocopying or any electronic or mechanical means, including information storage or retrieval systems, without permission in writing from both the copyright owner and the publisher of the book. The right of Frances E Wilson to be identified as the author of this work has been asserted by her in accordance with the Copyright, Designs, and Patents Act 1988 and any subsequent amendments thereto.

A catalogue record for this book is available from the British Library.

All Scripture unless otherwise stated have been taken from The Passion Translation version of the Bible

ISBN: 978-1-916801-35-6

1st Edition 2025 by Kingdom Publishers, London, UK.

You can purchase copies of this book from any leading bookstore or at:
www.kingdompublishers.co.uk

Acknowledgements

Scripture quotations are from The Passion Translation unless otherwise stated; scriptures marked NIV are from the New International Version, and AMP are from the Amplified version.

Emphasis within Scripture is the author's own.

All pronouns referring to the Father, Son, and Holy Spirit are capitalised and may differ from some Bible publishers' style. The name of satan and related names are not capitalised, as we choose not to acknowledge him, even to the point of violating grammatical rules.

My grateful thanks go to Di Patchett, who made time in her very busy schedule to correct all my many grammatical mistakes. Thanks so much.

I'm so indebted to Jane and Steve Adkin for providing me with such a peaceful home on their amazing farm and allowing me to stay 18 months longer than originally offered, with the result that I was able to write, without disturbance, but with beautiful scenery. It was there that I had the delightful experiences of lambing for the first time and also of God healing me after years of very limited mobility. Thank you all for your love and caring. May the farm continue to flourish both physically and spiritually.

My equally grateful thanks go to Peter who runs the most amazing IT distance rescue service for novices like me, actually just for me, as I really haven't a clue. Your patience, grace and determination to find a way, where there seems to be no way, have been outstanding. God bless you beyond your greatest dreams. Thank you so much for being a real friend.

Endorsements

Maybe you, like me, are not a visionary thinker. I was not a child who loved lots of free fanciful play, my mind is instead geared toward order and organisation, structure with a hearty dose of reality. Rarely do I let my imagination go wild and explore the avenues of wonder and transport myself to another world. I have, however, always wanted to do this when it comes to reading the Bible. I often have to remind myself that the Bible was written for me but not to me. I know that in order to understand it fully I must think more deeply, place myself within the context and commit to understanding the culture, the restrictions, the rules and the societal norms of the day. Fran's beautiful book has helped me immensely in this quest. By writing through the lens of the women who Jesus brought close to Him and exploring the many thoughts and challenges they would have been facing, it has helped me to gain greater understanding and empathy for those who were there. Those women who had the incredible privilege of being friends of Jesus. The Meditations for Holy week will draw you into the story as you allow yourself to sit in key narratives of what I believe to be the most life altering week in all of history. I pray that as you read this book you will shift your mindset from seeking knowledge and information to instead seeing aspects of yourself within the many women portrayed and find hope and comfort in the fact that Jesus loved them just as they were but also too much to let them stay that way. All these years later, He loves us just as we are and seeks to walk just as closely with us spiritually as he did with them when he was here in the flesh.

Naomi Murphy, senior pastor Life Church, Bedworth.

Fran has an amazing ability to see the stories we know so well in a new light. In this book she transports us to that first Easter and helps us to imagine what it was like for those there before, during and after the events of Good Friday and Resurrection Sunday. The questions she imagines them asking, we find ourselves asking; the things she describes them watching we find ourselves watching too. Easter becomes so real when we let Fran reveal it to us in an experiential way and with her beautiful use of language. This is a book, not only for Easter but, to be read reflectively again and again so that we capture the amazing gift from God that Easter is, and stir our hearts to offer greater levels of thankfulness to Jesus, the One who did it all for us.

Lorna Beedham, published poet, trustee Life Church, Bedworth

Contents

Yes, Who is This Jesus?
The Crib, the Cross and the Crown — 13

Chapter 1   It Was A Strange Time! — 16

Chapter 2   We Women Mingled… — 19

Chapter 3   Jesus Spent a Few Days Teaching... — 23

Chapter 4   We'd Missed Out.… — 29

Chapter 5   Standing a Little Way Off... — 31

Chapter 6   But Back To The Cross… — 34

Chapter 7   Here We Were Fairly Near... — 37

Chapter 8   What Happened in the Next Few Hours… — 40

Chapter 9   A Day or so Later ... — 45

Chapter 10   But Here We Are… — 48

Chapter 11   So, the First Part Was Being Fulfilled — 52

Peter's Dismay — 55

Pilate's Dilemma — 59

The Desperate Journey From the Cross to the Tomb — 65

The Divine Invitation — 67

GIVEN — 69

He Shed His Life-Giving Blood — 72

A Ponder Page — 74

Jesus' Dearest Desire, — 76

How Long? — 76

The Passion of The Christ — 79

About the Author — 83

Introduction

Who is This Jesus That Loved Us So Much?

Yes, Who is This Jesus? The Crib, the Cross and the Crown

Jesus crept out of heaven. No one on earth knew He'd left the amazing glory, honour, and adoration which He had enjoyed since before time began. Yes, He crept out of heaven and hid Himself, totally restricting Himself for nine months in the womb of Mary who, with the support of Joseph, was willing to provide that hiding place even though it cost her so dearly throughout her life.

And then Jesus came out of hiding. He revealed Himself to the world as a newborn babe, but immediately, as the custom was, He was restricted by others. He was wrapped in swaddling clothes, and laid in a manger, unable to move or do anything. In that situation, He was harmless. When we celebrate Christmas again, where is our Jesus? Is He wrapped in swaddling clothes and put in straw in an improvised manger, just as He was last year? And then, when we get to Twelfth Night, we wrap Him up even further. Oh yes, very carefully along with the other characters of that first Christmas in a black bin liner, and put Him back in the attic, hiding Him for another year.

Or is the Jesus, whose birth we may celebrate at Christmas, the appealing young man in a long flowing garment and sandals, 30 years old, who shows such love and compassion to the hungry, the sick, the poor, the downtrodden and the children?

Yes, we may be glad about His attitudes but restrict Him with scientific reasoning as to how He appeared to do some of the miracles. We restrict Him even more by reworking what He taught us, to fit in with our ideas so that it doesn't challenge our thinking or our lifestyle.

How restricted is our Jesus?
What is His clothing in our minds?

The soldiers showed very clearly what they thought of Jesus, they stripped Him of His long flowing garment, put a scarlet robe and a crown of thorns on Him. They beat Him, mocked Him horrendously, then they stripped Him again and put His own clothes back on as they led Him out. As they crucified Him, they stripped Him again, nailing Him to the Cross - could there be any greater restriction?

Yet there, in all that agony, He had absolute freedom to complete what He had come to earth for. No one was able to restrict Him from dying in our place. It is why He came to the Crib, in order to go to the Cross, and though two of His friends took Him down from the Cross and wrapped Him in adult swaddling clothes and laid Him in the tomb with such love and care, NO restrictions, not even the huge stone rolled in front of the tomb, sealed and guarded continuously by soldiers could prevent Him from rising from the dead and neatly leaving the linen clothes in the empty tomb.

Nothing and no one could restrict Him from appearing to the women in the garden early on Resurrection morning. Nothing and no one could restrict Him from appearing to many disciples during the next few days. Nothing and no one could restrict Him from returning to glory, to the amazing applause of heaven, for the mission completed and His crown restored.

Which is the Jesus we are celebrating today?

Jesus in swaddling clothes?
Jesus in His long flowing garment and sandals?
Jesus in a scarlet robe with a crown of thorns rammed on His head?
Jesus stripped and nailed to the Cross?
Jesus wrapped in grave clothes?
Jesus in His resurrection clothes?

OR…Jesus enthroned and re-clothed in all His splendour and glory, worshipped by myriads of angels while constantly interceding for each one of us?
Which is our personal Jesus?

He longs to open up each aspect of Himself to us personally, for the less restricted our understanding of Who He is and what He has done, the more real will be our personal celebration, day by day – be it Christmas, Easter, or Ascension, or any day in between.

He deliberately came to the Crib in order to go to the Cross, in order for us to have unrestricted access to Him in His glory as His sons and daughters.

Let's celebrate His birth, His life, His death, His resurrection, and His return to glory by giving Him unrestricted, unlimited access to our own personal lives.

Nothing will bring Him greater joy!

Come and meet the Jesus that we got to know and love and Who loved us so unconditionally.

Chapter 1
It Was A Strange Time!

It was a strange time! What was going on? We were excited but apprehensive. Was this the time when Jesus was going to make His Messiahship known publicly? We knew something was afoot but what?

We'd come to know Him during the last three years, though obviously, His mother, Mary and some of the others had known Him since He was born. We'd watched Him love the children, heal the sick, and release those held by demonic powers -what a change we'd seen in Mary Magdalene. Wow! We'd watched Him raise the dead, feed the multitudes and His teaching was SO different from that of the religious leaders. He talked a lot about His heavenly Father and wanted us to know Him too.

He honoured us as friends. Yes, us women! He didn't see us just as those who provided for the men - nice meals, homes, and care for the children. He honoured us. He showed us real respect, so different from the culture of our day.

He healed Peter's *mother-in-law*, He brought Jairus' *daughter* back to life, and He had such compassion on the *widow* of Nain that He brought her son back to life, even though he was on his way to be buried. He confirmed the faith of the *woman* who'd had a haemorrhage for 12 years when she touched the hem of His garment. Others would have scolded her for making Him unclean, but He honoured her and healed her. He healed the possessed *daughter* of the Syrophoenician *woman* when culturally He shouldn't even have spoken to her, or to the Samaritan *woman*, with whom He had a long, gracious conversation at the well of Sychar that changed her life and that of her whole village.

He honoured the women, who, in spite of the criticism of men, and even some of the disciples, used their life savings, their alabaster jars of perfume, to anoint Him and He defended their loving generosity from the mean comments of some of the guys.

We were such a mixed group of women; we came from different towns and villages around Galilee. We came from different backgrounds, and we all had our own story to tell of what Jesus had done for us, said to us, and meant to us.

For many of us, we'd met up on the mountain when Jesus was teaching for three days and we'd just stayed there listening, we didn't want to miss anything He said. They reckoned there were about 5000 men there, but Jesus wasn't just concerned for the men. He provided out of a little boy's lunch, enough bread and fish to feed at least 15000 when you count all the women and children, as well as, the men. It certainly was a family experience, one we talked about so many times while trying to get our heads around it.

We'd all sat down in our groups as the disciples told us to. Yes, we really were hungry, very hungry, but our minds were agog with all that Jesus had been teaching us over the past three days. We'd run out of food two days ago, we hadn't expected to stay more than the first day, it was all unscripted, nothing arranged. You don't take three days' worth of food when you are only going for a day. What was happening? Why weren't we being sent home or to the nearby villages to buy food? Why were we sitting down?

Then one of the disciples came to our group - he had bread and fish in his hands - well that wasn't going to go very far between the 50 people in our group! Or…was it? As he gave a portion to the person nearest to him what was left in his hands remained the same, he just kept on giving it out, *bread and fish, bread and fish, bread and fish* for everyone, more than we could eat. "Where did this come from?" we asked His disciple, and he answered, "A young lad gave Jesus his lunch, five loaves and two small fish. We said to Him, 'What use is that among so many?' but He received what was offered, and gave thanks to His Father for it and this is the result, you are all having an amazing free meal!"

Well, you can imagine what it was like when we started walking down the mountain back home, everyone was talking to everyone. I was talking to women I'd never even seen before let alone talked to, but what happened was so unifying that whenever we recognised anyone from the gathering, we'd start talking – yes, mainly about Jesus.

As a result, many of us welcomed Him into our homes when He came to our own villages. We felt it such an honour to have Him come, and it was our honour to minister to His practical needs as best we could, after all, He'd ministered to our practical, emotional and spiritual needs.

And so, as the weeks turned into months and then into a few years, the group of women who ministered to Him grew, not only because He fed us, but because we knew He loved and honoured us. To Him we were not second-class citizens, we mattered, as did the children. Strangely, as we ministered to Him in whatever way we could instead of competing with each other, our friendships grew to such an extent that when He set out to go to Jerusalem for the last time we went together. Somehow, we knew it was crucial that we went even though none of us knew why.

As we got nearer to Jerusalem, a long 70 mile walk from Galilee which took a few days, we somehow managed to keep up with Jesus and His disciples, did they go more leisurely for our sake? I don't really think so because Jesus had set His face like a flint to go and He needed to be there at the right moment, whenever that was. As we got nearer, other women joined us who'd ministered to Him when He had come up to Jerusalem on other occasions. There was Mary, Cleopas' wife, who lived in Emmaus about 7 miles outside Jerusalem, and then He loved to go to Mary, Martha and Lazarus' home in Bethany as well.

There were so many of us, it was almost like a 'fan club' but yet it wasn't at all. Yes, each of us would do anything we possibly could for Him, but it wasn't immature infatuation, most of us were mature women, many with adult children, including Zebedee's wife, James and John's mother, and Mary Magdalene and many others.

We just so appreciated the honour, the love, the caring, and the respect He had shown each of us and this was our spontaneous response to go with Him to Jerusalem and make sure everything was as good as it could be for Him. We knew that something different was about to happen though we certainly didn't know what.

Chapter 2

We Women Mingled...

We women mingled with the crowd as Jesus rode into Jerusalem on the donkey. Palm branches were being waved by the crowd and thrown onto the path as well as people throwing their cloaks down for the donkey to walk on. It was only an unbroken colt in the middle of an ecstatic crowd, so noisy, so excited, shouting at the top of their voices, "Hosanna to the Son of David," "Blessed be the King who comes in the name of the Lord," "Hosanna in the highest heaven." To begin with, we were afraid for Jesus' safety, would the colt freak out and throw Him off? We should have known better by now. Jesus was in control; the colt was completely unfazed. Jesus was 'on board' so he could walk without fear through chaos and noise. He obviously *knew* that Jesus was in complete control, both of the crowd and himself, never would that colt forget that amazing experience and the honour of being the one that Jesus chose to ride.

Oh, that I would always remember that Jesus is still in complete control, no matter what is going on around me, so long as I allow Him to hold the reins and direct my path. With Him 'on board' I have no need, no right, to fear or freak out and, may I say it ever so gently, nor have you.

Am I, are you, allowing Him to direct the path we tread, and dictate the speed at which we tread it? If we do, He will give us experiences and privileges we've never dreamt of. Isn't it amazing that however wild, unbroken, or even broken we may be, Jesus very gently, wants to 'ride' our lives with us and steer us through all that would entangle our feet, distract, or frighten us.

But to get back to the story...we weren't the only ones going up to Jerusalem, it was Passover time, so great crowds were going up to celebrate this most special feast. It was the busiest time of the year in the City, with people coming from all over the known world to worship, so we were not obvious, we just blended in with all the other visitors.

Having ridden into Jerusalem Jesus went to the Temple. He knew all the fraudulent goings on in there. He knew how the poor, the ones who could only afford pigeons for sacrifices, were being fleeced when they came up to worship. How the only court we women could go to worship in, had become like an animal market where the rates of exchange, from ordinary currency to Temple currency, were extortionate and totally unjust, far worse than the ordinary tax collectors cheating on us.

Because this was going on in the Women's Court, we were able to see what was happening. The men normally went straight through there into the Men's Court but we watched in amazement, horror, delight, and a whole lot of other very mixed emotions as Jesus, with very controlled, authoritative anger, strode in there and tipped up all the tables, scattering money, birds and animals everywhere while declaring, "My house shall be called a House of Prayer for all nations, but you have made it a den of thieves."

No sooner had Jesus done that than we saw an amazing contrast happen. The lame and the blind came to Jesus in the Temple porches. Yes, despite them and their 'carers' sensing how angry He was, they felt it was safe for them to come to Him, and indeed it was safe. He healed each one and while He was ministering to them, the children who were watching them, started to shout what they had heard when Jesus rode in on the colt, "Hosanna to the son of David." It was a beautiful scene, the blind seeing, the lame walking, running, jumping, and the children shouting Jesus' praise.

Yet, behind that oasis arose black storm clouds of anger and hatred, as the Chief Priests and scribes saw what was happening and hated it. They tried to trick Jesus with their questions but they couldn't. He always outwitted them even though He wasn't trying to score points. He was explaining to them in parables or stories how, in spite of all their religiosity, they were missing the boat completely. He told so many stories to help them understand. Indeed, having left the temple and gone out to Bethany for the night, He came back the next morning and continued to tell more and more stories. The more stories He told, the angrier the religious leaders became, because they knew by now that He was talking about them. They weren't about to change their minds, let alone their hearts, not even when He said they were like white-washed sepulchres, beautiful on the outside but full of dead men's bones and everything impure on the inside. They were SO livid, SO jealous and by now SO determined to silence Him but they were afraid, yes, afraid of us the ordinary people.

They knew from His ride into Jerusalem, if not before, how much we loved Him. Why? Because He SO loved us, unlike the leaders who showed no love or concern for those they were supposed to lead to God. They treated us with such contempt and arrogance, while He treated us with such honour, even the woman caught in adultery by those leaders who wanted to stone her. He honoured her, He didn't embarrass her any more than she was already embarrassed, He didn't look her in the face accusingly, He looked down and wrote in the sand. I always wondered what He wrote but my friend was crying so much she couldn't read it. Was He just doodling, or was He writing the names of the religious leader's mistresses or something completely different? Whatever He wrote, He spoke very directly to the leaders, who were like a pack of angry wolves ready to tear their prey to pieces, saying, "Whoever of you is without sin let him cast the first stone."

There was silence, then dull thud after dull thud as each man, starting with the eldest first, let their rock drop to the ground beside them. Full of embarrassment, they left the scene as inconspicuously as possible, and pretty soon there was only Jesus and the woman left. He asked her, "Where are your accusers? Has no one condemned you?" She looked around very timidly, still expecting a missile to come hurtling at her but there was nobody there, only a crowd of rocks. Gasping in amazement she replied "No one, Lord." "Then neither do I condemn you, go and sin no more," Jesus replied so gently, with such compassion. He knew how traumatised she was, He knew how unfair all this had been, He knew how terrified she'd been. He made it plain that in no way did He condemn her but asked her not to sin again. She knew He had forgiven her, she knew He understood the whole situation, she knew He was giving her a new beginning, she knew He honoured her and respected her in spite of her sin.

This is why we women loved Him and honoured Him and delighted to provide for Him as and when we could, because no matter who we were or what our circumstances, He loved and honoured us. He specially honoured the little old widow who came to the Temple while He was there to put into the coffers her last two tiny coins, all that she had. She gave out of her devotion to God, even though she had nothing else to live on, unlike the other folk who were making a great performance of giving their gifts which were only a tiny percentage of their wealth. As Jesus said they got their praise from men, but the widow got none from men but much from God. Jesus saw her heart and loved her devotion and generosity, her self-denial and her hunger to please God. Jesus also saw the hearts of the wealthy givers – pompous, praise-seeking and mean.

This was a wonderful, but sometimes scary, thing about Jesus that we had come to discover. Without us saying anything He could read our hearts; He knew our motives often better than we knew them ourselves. He also knew the hearts of those who criticised us for ministering to Him, and when appropriate would even defend us women in public.

Because He could read us like an open book it caused us to be careful in our relationships with each other.

> How could we dishonour those He honoured?
> How could we dislike those He readily loved?
> How could we be dispassionate to those
> He had so much compassion for?

Chapter 3
Jesus Spent a Few Days Teaching...

Yes, Jesus spent a few days teaching in the Temple Court, telling stories that we could all understand, although at the time we didn't always realise the implications of what He was saying. In the evenings He would go back to Bethany and stay with Simon the Leper, or should we call him Simon, The-Once-Was-A-Leper, or with Mary, Martha and Lazarus. It was from Bethany that He quietly gave instructions to two of His disciples about how to find the right house, in which to prepare the Passover meal for Him to eat with His disciples.

They were to go into the City and follow a man carrying a water jar and ask to speak to the owner of the house he went into. It was unheard of for men to carry the water jars, it was always we women who had to carry the heavy vessels, either on our shoulders or on our heads, men just didn't carry them.

The instructions for these disciples were very simple, to find the one man who would stand out in a crowd if you knew you were looking for him. The issue would be timing. If the two disciples took a circuitous route or visited a friend on the way, they would no doubt have missed the water carrier. But Jesus' timing was always spot on, He was never late and never early. We thought He was very late when Lazarus died. Jesus didn't come for four days, even though He knew he was so ill and then had died. He could have come earlier and healed Him while he was still alive like He had others, but NO. He made sure that everyone knew that Lazarus was well and truly dead. Why? So that everyone would know that he had been well and truly raised from the dead, and give glory to God.

Jesus' choreography of situations was amazing. He appeared to be so laid back, and yet everything happened with the precision timing of heaven. How had His timing appeared at the beginning of His ministry, after He went to Simon Peter's home and his mother-in-law was desperately ill with a fever, not the time to visit, or was it? Jesus immediately healed her and she got straight up and ministered to Him.

What about the timing with Jairus, whose daughter was dying and on the way, Jesus stopped and allowed Himself to be interrupted by a woman who, on touching the hem of His garment, was instantly healed. He could have ignored her as He was on an important mission to heal this dying girl but no, He took the time to confirm the woman's faith. He sent her home with His blessing of peace, or the peace of His blessing. But how frustrating for Jairus, how desperate he must have felt. As a ruler of the synagogue, he wasn't used to being kept waiting, especially in this situation where every minute mattered and now they came and told him that his daughter was dead, so not to trouble Jesus, it was too late.

But Jesus wasn't flustered or apologetic, all He said was, "Do not fear, only believe," and kept walking to Jairus' home where He turned out the professional mourners, who were weeping and wailing, and went into where the dead 12-year-old was lying, took her by the hand and said to her, "Little lamb, it's time to get up." And immediately she stood up and walked, and He gave her back to her parents, telling them to give her something to eat.

Why didn't Jesus get there in time to heal her? I guess it was about the 'Greater Glory' as with Lazarus. He was in control. He knew what the timing needed to be for the greater glory to be seen. But sometimes it was very hard for us 'normal mortals' to understand Jesus' timing. The disciples often asked Him, "When shall this be?" as He told them about things that would happen in the future, some in the *very* near future, and some in the much more distant future.

As I look back on our history, God's timing is amazing with the right people, in the right place, with the right condition of heart, ready to do His will at the right time. Yet He often went to extremes for the timing to be right:

- Joseph was in prison for 13 years before ruling in Egypt
- David was anointed as a very young lad but not crowned as king for years

- Esther waited for three years to fulfil her God-given mission
- Moses was 40 years in the palace, and 40 years in the desert before leading the people out of slavery in Egypt.

And then I remember hearing of God's amazing timing with Elisabeth and Zechariah, just 33 years ago, way past childbearing age, but their son John was born just at the right time, to be the herald for Jesus. I guess I never really will understand God's timing in my life, in the nation's life, and in the world's life but I know that He is always on time otherwise He wouldn't be God.

By definition, God cannot be late or early,
He's always on time.

When I remember that, it's a huge relief when things are difficult and don't seem to be coming together. Sometimes I think we can keep Him waiting by *our* not being ready or willing to do what He wants us to, when He wants us to do 'it'. Just like Jonah not being willing to go to Nineveh, he delayed God's timing by going in the opposite direction.

On the other hand, at the wedding in Cana where Jesus was a guest, it seems that Mary, His mother, brought His miracles forward. When she told Him that the wine had run out at the feast, He said, "What has that got to do with Me? My time has not yet come." And then He promptly turned gallons and gallons of foot-washing water into the most beautiful wine, enough to set the young couple up in business for life, as well as quench the thirst of the guests.

But to get back to the two disciples, they saw the water carrier and followed him just as Jesus had instructed them and the master of the house had the room ready for them so that they could prepare for the Passover meal on that Thursday evening. For some reason way back in our history, Galileans celebrated Passover on Thursday evening while the rest of Israel celebrated it on Friday. We didn't understand the significance of the timing till after the weekend, but it meant that Jesus could celebrate Passover. This became SO important as He elevated it to something so much greater than just the yearly remembrance of the Exodus of our people from slavery in Egypt. On the day, as the sacrificial Passover lambs were being slaughtered in the Temple, He, the Lamb of God, chose to be slaughtered, at exactly the same time, between the sixth and the nineth hours (12.00 noon - 3.00 pm)

The disciples told us later what had happened at their Passover meal with Jesus. How He had taken the middle slice of unleavened bread out of the bag, blessed it, and gave it to His disciples saying, "This is My body given for you, do this in remembrance of Me." When the meal ended, He took the fourth cup of wine which they had, blessed it and said, "Drink you all of it, this is My blood of the New Covenant which is poured out for many for the forgiveness of sins."

By being crucified, as He was, He not only fulfilled so many prophecies in our Scriptures but He also took the place, *once and for all*, of the sacrifices that we had been commanded through Moses to make.

> He became our Atonement, our burnt offering,
> our sin offering for unintentional sin,
> our guilt offering
> and our Passover Lamb.

Under Moses what you brought for your sacrifice depended on how wealthy or poor you were. When you were bringing a sin offering or a guilt offering and were wealthy, you could be proud at the same time, but if you were poor and could only afford a couple of pigeons or a cereal offering, you just felt so humiliated. Either way, it became very hard to focus on why we were making the offering, but now Jesus is our final, complete guilt offering. He has offered His whole self for each of us. To Him we are all worth dying for but all equally guilty. It cost Him the same for each one of us, whether we are wealthy or poor, whether we are 'morally good' or a hardened criminal, or anywhere in between.

I'm reminded of what God spoke through Isaiah (one of our amazing prophets of long ago), when he so accurately prophesied exactly what Jesus would go through, in Isaiah 53:6 (KJV), and why. But what was the why? "…because ALL we like sheep have gone astray, we have turned everyone to his own way and the Lord has laid on Him the iniquity of us".

Then a bit later on, in Isaiah 64:6 (KJV), he says, "ALL our righteousness's are as filthy rags." Yes, in God's sight, we've all gone our own way and even our very best, no matter who we are, is like filthy rags to Him, and that's why we so badly needed a sin and a guilt offering that was completely adequate, *"Once and for All."*

When we heard Jesus cry out on the cross as He was about to die, "It is finished," we women, who were looking on from a distance, assumed that He meant His life was finished, His attempt to set us free from Roman occupation was finished, His attempt to be King of the Jews was finished, and that His attempt to be Messiah had finished. It was all so strange, so confusing. Here was the man so many of us had come to love and trust, whom we'd seen heal the sick, cast out demons, raise the dead, love the children, feed the hungry, and honour us women, now dying, crucified on a cross – the punishment reserved for the worst criminals, crying out, "It is finished," by which we understood He meant, "It's over, I've failed, it's the end."

How could this be? How could someone who could raise the dead fail to be what He claimed to be? Our hearts were broken, was it all trickery? NO! We knew all He'd done was real. Nothing could change that, but now He was dying right in front of our eyes. Yes, we were standing at a distance, but near enough to see and hear what was going on. Our hearts were just torn for His mother Mary, His brothers and sisters, the other Mary and John, and that's why we left them a bit of space near the Cross.

We were willing Him to get off the cross and prove who He was, but He didn't, instead, He cried out, "It is finished," and gave up His life. We had to assume that that was the end, that our lives would revert to where they were before we met Jesus. It was going to be very strange and not at all easy to write off the last three years of our lives, as a complete illusion, and endure the mocking that was sure to come our way from those who'd never believed Him.

We hung out with His disciples as it was Passover and the Sabbath so we couldn't travel back to Galilee straight away, and anyhow, as soon as we were allowed by law we'd go to the tomb where Joseph and Nicodemus had buried Jesus' body. We wanted to make sure they'd done everything properly, you know how we women are.

Chapter 4
We'd Missed Out....

Yes, we'd missed out on Thursday night and weren't going to miss out on anything else. We'd assumed that after they'd had the Passover meal together and gone to the Mount of Olives that Jesus and the disciples would make their way back to Bethany, as on the previous nights and that Jesus would resume teaching in the Temple on Friday morning. It wasn't till very early that morning that we heard what a horrendous night it had been for Jesus and the disciples, and then we women joined in the most horrendously imaginable day possible.

Late on Thursday night, Jesus was betrayed by Judas in the Garden of Gethsemane and taken to the Chief Priests. They then took Him to Pilate very early on Friday morning demanding His crucifixion.

The crowd, which had been so friendly, so excited when Jesus rode into Jerusalem was now so hostile, baying like a huge pack of hungry wolves. Every time Pilate came out and spoke to the public saying that he could find no fault in Jesus and wanting to let Him go they just screamed out, "Crucify Him, crucify Him!" After trying many times to let Jesus go free, he gave in to the savage demands of the crowd who had been whipped into a frenzy by the Chief Priests and Pharisees.

We were on the edge of the crowd, it certainly wasn't safe to be in the middle of it, and we were praying like we'd never prayed before, praying the prayer that Jesus Himself had taught us when the disciples had asked Him to teach us to pray. Yes, we prayed with all our might, "Our Father in heaven, hallowed, holy is Your name. Your kingdom come, Your will be done here on earth as it is in heaven." We were desperate to see God the Father's will be done in this situation. His will must be the safe release of Jesus. It couldn't be His will for Jesus to be treated in this way. It couldn't be His will for Jesus to be crucified.

We later learnt, probably from young John Mark's mother what Jesus had prayed in the Garden before He was arrested. John Mark records in his gospel the incident of a young man who was watching but hiding, and then had to run, shaking off his sheet when the rabble tried to arrest him too. Anyhow, even though James, Peter and John, whom Jesus had asked especially to watch and pray with Him while He went a bit further on, fell asleep three times, yes, *three times,* someone heard Jesus cry out three times, "Father, if it be possible let this cup pass from Me, nevertheless not My will but Yours be done."

Wasn't this what we were praying too?

It's just in retrospect that we realised that Jesus really knew what Father's will was. We thought we knew but we were completely wrong, but Father did answer our prayers and caused His will to be done.

We gasped as we saw Jesus being led out by the soldiers, struggling under the weight of the crossbeam on His back and shoulders which had been torn to shreds from the early morning flogging administered by the tough burly soldiers. They delighted in mocking Him and rammed a 'crown' of thorns on His head. Blood was everywhere, down His back and His face. We longed to help Him but knew we wouldn't be allowed to, but were relieved when Simon of Cyrene was forced to carry the crossbeam for Jesus. We were crying so much, heartbroken that all this was happening to our beloved Friend, knowing that it was all completely unjustified, He had done nothing wrong.

By now there was a great crowd of us, the angry mob seemed to have melted away somewhat, and in the middle of all His agony, mental, physical, and emotional, He turned His loving gaze on us. His voice weak, He said, "Daughters of Jerusalem don't weep for Me, weep for yourselves and your children..." and He warned us of the awful times to come. As usual, we didn't understand but were amazed at His caring for us as women, in the midst of this terrible situation which He knew, and we knew, was about to get even worse as they led Him out of the City to Golgotha, the Place of the Skull, where they would crucify Him, right beside the main thoroughfare for all to see as they passed by.

Chapter 5
Standing a Little Way Off...

Yes, here we were standing a little way off from the Cross, but we could hear and see, except at midday when everything went pitch dark, what was going on? Not only darkness, but earthquakes as well, it was terrifying. We huddled together hardly daring to breathe, wondering whatever would happen next, listening intently as every so often during those three hours Jesus spoke out – cried out.

Once He spoke to His mother Mary and John, the beloved disciple, arranging for him to take real care of her, it was as if He was hugging them both with His heart, even though His arms were pinned to the Cross.

Once He spoke to the thief on the cross next to Him, who somehow had realised more about Jesus than we had, because he said to Jesus, "Remember me when You come into your kingdom, when you come into your kingly glory." What did this guy know about Jesus? Was it just that he'd heard people read the plaque over Jesus' head that Pilate had insisted on writing, and would not allow to be changed even though the Chief Priests demanded change? "NO," said Pilate, "What I have written I have written," which was "Jesus, king of the Jews."

Everyone could read it as they passed by, and hundreds were passing by because it was Passover time. Was that how this criminal knew that Jesus indeed had a kingdom, one that He was about to enter? We hadn't realised that. In fact, all our hopes of Jesus having a kingdom were completely shattered, they were nailed to the Cross with Him. Was it that Jesus was behaving in such a different way from himself and the other criminal, even though He was in the same terrible, excruciating situation? Did he understand Jesus' reply, "Today you will be with Me in Paradise?"

We certainly didn't understand, did Paradise equal the grave, death, and the end of life? It definitely didn't look as if it was going to be somewhere lovely. All that lay ahead of them as far as we and the two criminals knew, was death followed by being thrown into a pauper's grave in a hurry because Passover would begin at sundown that evening.

How did this criminal know that Jesus had "done nothing amiss?" Had he, previous to being caught and tried, watched Jesus in action? Healing the sick, raising the dead, feeding the hungry, loving the children? Had he yearned to be a disciple but struggled to leave his old life, not realising that Jesus would enable him as He had other disciples, and many of us women too? The wonder of the situation was that this hardened, or not so hardened, criminal spent the last couple of hours of his earthly life knowing that Jesus had accepted him. Knowing that he had been received by the King of the Jews unconditionally, in spite of all he'd been and done. Apart from all the physical agony of crucifixion that he was enduring he must have been overloaded with such a mixture of emotions. The amazing joy of being accepted by Jesus and the promise of spending eternity with Him, with the deep regret of leaving it till the last minute to get right with Him, when he could possibly have done that much earlier during the last three years of his life, once Jesus had become publicly known for His teaching, His compassion and His miracles.

Like He did Mary and John, like He did those of us He called 'Daughters of Jerusalem', Jesus also embraced this criminal. Who else can embrace you while He's nailed to a cross in such physical but also spiritual agony? Only Jesus.

We heard Him cry out, "My God, My God why have You forsaken Me?" Yes, why had God His Father, whom He had always honoured and spoken so highly of to us, and with whom He was in constant communication, saying, "I only do what I see My Father doing," forsaken Jesus now and let this terrible situation arise? We had been told that when He was baptised, Father had spoken from heaven saying in a loud voice, "This is My beloved Son in whom I am well pleased." We later learnt that when Peter, James and John were up the mountain, Moses and Elijah appeared with Jesus, who was transfigured before them and Father spoke very clearly from heaven saying, "This is My beloved Son. Listen to Him." Jesus forbade them to speak about this encounter till after His resurrection and they'd managed to keep quiet, not understanding what Jesus was intimating, and nor would we have done.

But why did Father turn His back on His beloved Son at this crucial time? We didn't understand till sometime later that Jesus was becoming our sin offering and our guilt offering, carrying all our sins and Father couldn't look at that.

In addition He also became our Passover Lamb. The lamb was killed, and it's blood was shed so that everyone in the household was saved from slavery and death. Jesus chose to be killed as our final Passover Lamb so that we could be saved from eternal death, life in hell forever, and slavery now in bondage to satan. Only He as the pure, spotless Lamb of God could do this and He chose to do so at such amazing, indescribable cost – separation from His beloved Father, with whom He had always had complete unity - until the sacrifice was complete.

No wonder He cried out, "Why have you forsaken Me?"

We understood this so much better when Mary, Cleopas' wife, shared with us what happened as they walked home so dejectedly from Jerusalem to Emmaus, about seven miles, on the evening of the first day of the week after the Crucifixion. They were joined by a man who asked them why they were so sad. They explained to Him what had happened and then the stranger opened up all the Scriptures showing them why Christ the Messiah had to die. He showed how Jesus had completed all the required blood sacrifices, and that each one was a copy, a type, to show us what Jesus had done. It was an amazing seven-mile Bible study.

But it wasn't until He agreed to come in and have a meal with them, as per our Jewish custom we always have to invite strangers in for a meal or the night if it's late, and He took the bread and blessed it and broke it and then vanished out of their sight that they suddenly knew why their hearts had been burning within them. It was Jesus, the Risen Jesus, the Risen from the dead Jesus, who had just given them the most eye-opening, jaw-dropping, mind-blowing Bible study, they or anyone else had ever been part of. We could have been jealous but they came running straight back seven miles that night and shared it all with us.

Oh yes! It all began to make sense then.

Chapter 6
But Back To The Cross...

Yes, back to the Cross...

Maybe the cry I remember most, was Jesus calling out, "Father forgive them, they don't know what they are doing." What sort of request was that? Was He asking Father to forgive the Roman soldiers who had just flogged Him, mocked Him, nailed Him to the Cross, dropped it into the socket in the ground without any concern as to how much it shattered His body, and were now casting lots for His clothes? Yes, He probably was, but we thought they certainly knew what they were doing.

Was He asking Father to forgive the Chief Priests and Jewish leaders who hated Jesus, and had been so determined to get rid of Him and had incited the people to demand His Crucifixion? Yes, He probably was, but we thought they certainly knew what they were doing.

Was He asking Father to forgive the fickle crowd who had applauded His entry into Jerusalem on the colt but in the last few days had allowed themselves to be whipped up into a frenzy of hatred against Jesus? Yes, He probably was but we certainly thought they knew what they were doing.

Was He asking Father to forgive us women and the disciples for not standing up against this hatred and opposition? Yes, He probably was, in fact, I'm sure He was and it's true we didn't know what we were doing. We didn't know how to stand against the crowd, we didn't know this was all going to end in His Crucifixion.

Peter didn't know what he was doing warming himself by the enemies' fire late on Thursday night, that it would lead to denying ever having known Jesus before cock crow early on Friday morning.

What did Jesus mean when He said to Father, "They don't know what they are doing?" In one sense we all knew what we were doing, and we had various reasons for doing what we did, hatred, anger, jealousy, fear and so on but actually from Jesus' point of view, He knew that none of us understood the part we were playing in Jesus fulfilling all the prophecies, concerning Himself, His death and resurrection.

Not that I believe He forced any of us to do what we did but because He is omniscient, He knew what we would do, what choices we would make in each situation. Before He even created the universe and put into action the 'Rescue Plan', He and Father had already devised, knowing that each one of us would need a "Once and for All" sin offering, a "Once and for all" guilt offering, and a "Once and for All" Passover Lamb. Not that we would then have the liberty to sin as much as we wanted. Oh **NO**, when I realise what it cost Jesus to be my sin-and-guilt-offering and to be my Passover Lamb so that I can really experience Father's forgiveness and know that I have eternal life with them now, and equally when I die physically, it makes me desire not to sin, not to grieve Him, not to take any of what He has done for me, lightly, or for granted.

"Oh, thank you Jesus for asking Father to forgive us. Thank you, Father, that because of what Jesus did on the Cross and by rising from the dead, You can and do forgive us whenever we confess our sin, whatever shape or form it has taken. But Holy Spirit I ask that You give me an increasing hatred of sinning and an increasing love of obeying."

As I thought over this cry during the next days, months and years, I came to realise that this was the prayer I so often needed to pray when others hurt me, or those that I love. When I see injustice being meted out to those that I don't necessarily know. When people still mock Jesus.

It is often a real challenge to cry out and mean, "Father forgive them, they don't know what they are doing," but do you know that whenever I do that it takes away the bitterness, resentment and hatred in my heart? If I receive it, the Holy Spirit will replace those emotions with love for the perpetrators and that stops whatever they have done from having any more negative effects in my own life. When I release them, I am released, and that is wonderful because I no longer carry the burden or grudge.

> When I release them to You,
> You release me from them.

But back to the Cross.......

As I've already shared with you Jesus cried out, "It is finished, into Your hands I commit My spirit," and He died. We thought that He was admitting failure when He cried, "It is finished," but those who were standing nearer the Cross were adamant that it was a cry of triumph. At that exact moment, the most amazing thing happened. Remember that even though it was only three o'clock in the afternoon, it was pitch dark everywhere, except in the Temple where the seven-branched candlestick shed a little flickering light around in the Holy Place.

At that very moment Jesus cried out triumphantly, "It is finished," and chose to die, at that *very* moment, the veil in the Temple, the enormous 4-inch thick, 30-foot wide and 60-foot high curtain, was torn in two, from top to bottom and the inner-most room, the Holy of Holies, where God dwelt and only the High Priest could go to make atonement for the people with a sin offering once a year, was now open.

There was no longer a dividing wall between God and the people. Jesus had become the final sin offering so that through Him we could have direct access to our Holy God. We no longer had to wait until the Day of Atonement, or the Day of At-One-Ment as my children used to call it, when for maybe a few hours, we were 'at one' – right – with God. Then we had to remember all the sins we had accumulated for a whole year so that the High Priest could go into the Holy of Holies on our behalf, with the sin offering for next year. It was a burden to keep a year's record of my sin. It did act as a deterrent to sinning but nothing like the deterrent of knowing that Jesus had deliberately chosen to become my sin offering and my guilt offering to 'Atone' for me with Almighty God, my heavenly Father.

Knowing that and appreciating what He did for me personally, as well as for everyone else, has made me want to please Him more and more, honour Him more and more by obeying Him and sin less and less, but we didn't understand any of this until a few days later.

Chapter 7
Here We Were Fairly Near...

Yes, here we were fairly near the foot of the Cross with Jesus' dead body still on it. The other two criminals were still struggling to live or die and we were struggling to make any sense of all that had happened and, indeed, was still happening.

It was the day of preparation for the Passover Sabbath, a very important day so the Jewish leaders asked Pilate to order the legs of the criminals to be broken so that they'd die more quickly and the bodies could be taken away before the Sabbath began. The soldiers came and broke the legs of the first one, and then the other. Oh, how that hurt, we felt it too - but when they came to do the same to Jesus they realised He was already dead so they didn't break His legs, which fulfilled another prophecy which said, "Not one bone of His body was broken," but we watched in agonizing horror as one of the soldiers pierced His side and out flowed blood and water, a sign that He was truly dead. He had even chosen at what moment to die so that they did not break His legs but only pierce His side, fulfilling more prophecies as we came to understand later, but at the time it was so excruciating for all of us.

Strangely we gained a crumb of comfort from the Centurion who was keeping guard over Jesus and the other two. He had observed everything that had happened, including the earthquakes and was himself terrified, but as he watched Jesus and observed that He had already died in an unusually short space of time, he said, "Truly this was the Son of God."

Here was someone who hadn't known Jesus like we had but in this short but horrendous encounter, had recognised that here before him was someone very, very special. Someone who had been so dignified through all the ghastly procedure. Someone who cared for His Mother in the middle of His agony. Someone who chose to forgive all those who had a part in this whole 'charade', including himself casting lots for His clothes.

Someone who chose to die of His own free will, this was unheard of in the centurion's experience so he concluded that Jesus must be the Son of God. In our anguish and despair that was a comfort.

And then there was another slight comfort or rather relief. Joseph of Arimathea had the courage to go to Pilate and ask permission to take the body of Jesus and bury it. It was a very courageous thing to do as a member of the Jewish council who had demanded Jesus' death. He hadn't managed to stand against them, but now he was willing to do whatever he could and along with Nicodemus, who had been so afraid of what others thought of him that he'd come to Jesus by night when he wouldn't be seen, they came and received the body of Jesus from the Cross.

They anointed it with a large mixture of myrrh and aloes, wrapped it in linen clothes that were used for burial, and carried His body to a tomb in a nearby garden that had never been used. We suspected that it was a tomb Joseph had already prepared for his own burial and that of his family, for that's what rich people do in our culture. Joseph must have thought he'd given the tomb to Jesus for life, well for death, but actually, Jesus only borrowed it for three days! But Joseph didn't know that till later. So we followed him and Nicodemus as they carried Jesus to the tomb. We saw the tomb and how they laid Him in it and how they rolled a huge stone in front of the doorway so that no one could get in.

We discovered later that Pilate gave permission to the Jewish leaders to put a seal on the tomb and put a continuous guard there as well, because they remembered that Jesus had said, "After three days I will rise again." Although they didn't believe Him, they were very frightened that some of the disciples would come and steal His body away, claiming He had risen.

So, we went back to where we were staying to prepare more spices for burial that we would bring on the first day of the week as we were not allowed to do anything on the Sabbath, not even prepare spices, but as soon as Sabbath ended at 6.00 pm, we went into overdrive preparing the ointments and spices. We were so traumatised by all the barbaric brutality we had seen inflicted on our dearest Friend and by the destruction of all our hopes, dreams and indeed beliefs for the future, our own future, and the future of our nation, with Jesus being our Messiah, the King of the Jews, freeing us from the rule of Rome.

The spices were unintentionally diluted with 'gallons' of tears as our numbness would suddenly erupt into uncontrollable weeping, inconsolable grief, as the centre of our universe had been obliterated, snatched from us, annihilated. We could identify a bit with Rachel weeping for her children when Herod had ordered the massacre of all the boys, of two years old and under when he heard about Jesus from the Wise Men and was determined that He would not live to be King of the Jews. - That only happened about 31 years ago so it was very much in our current history when Jesus was about two years old.

Yes, it was our story,
but more importantly
it was His-story.

His story changed the entire history of the world, even the year numbers are changed because of Jesus' death and resurrection. The years are now known as BC - Before Christ - and AD - Ano Domini -the year of our Lord. But, on that Sabbath day we had NO clue about any of that, we thought, assumed, that Jesus' story had ended, just as He had cried out, "It is finished." He'd meant that it was over.

So mechanically, we did what we could to be ready for the morning. Our hearts were certainly overruling our heads. It hadn't crossed our minds to consider how we women would roll the huge stone away from the entrance of the tomb, even if the soldiers would let us and that was doubtful.

Our hearts were so full of so many different emotions...grief, anger, hatred, love, compassion, bewilderment, fear, emptiness, and disappointment that it was nigh impossible to engage the brain, we were just functioning on autopilot. So in that state, before dawn, deprived of two nights' sleep, and drained of gallons of tears, we set off to the tomb with all the spices we had prepared.

Chapter 8

What Happened in the Next Few Hours...

What happened in the next few hours was beyond our wildest dreams or imagination, so forgive me, if at times I seem to be a bit confused as to what happened when, and in what order who met who!

As far as I remember we women, Mary Magdalene, Joanna, Mary the mother of James and Salome, and several others, were on our way to the tomb, very early, when suddenly there was this terrific earthquake. It really frightened all of us so much that we stopped in our tracks, wondering what would happen next. After all, on Friday, there had been that big earthquake and the veil of the Temple had been torn in two, from the top to the bottom. So what was this quake? Was it just a natural occurrence or did this have something to do with Jesus? Anyhow, Mary Magdalene, frightened though she was, was so concerned about Jesus' body, worried that it had been damaged in the quake, that she ran as fast as she could to the tomb. Upon arriving, she went straight into the tomb, forgetting that there should have been a huge stone across the entrance. She ran straight out again crying, "They've taken away my Lord and I don't know where they've laid Him," because there was no body there. She went as fast as she could into the City to find the disciples and tell them that Jesus' body was missing.

In the meantime, we continued to the garden in a very fearful manner. Afraid because of the earthquakes and possible aftershocks, and afraid at the thought of the soldiers guarding the tomb, knowing they might treat us women very roughly. Would we be able to move the stone, and would we even be allowed in, to get to the body of our dear Friend to anoint it further?

As we turned the corner and faced the tomb, we were so glad to find that there were no guards there, they had fled in fear.

The stone was to the side of the entrance, so we had free access but then we gasped and stopped in our tracks, terrified at finding an angel sitting on top of it. His appearance was like lightning and His garment as white as snow. He told us not to be alarmed or frightened. He knew we were looking for Jesus who had been crucified, and he told us that He was not here, but He had risen, as He had said He would do. The angel then invited us to go into the tomb to see where Jesus' body had been placed. Inside, there were two more of these dazzling angels who asked us, "Why are you seeking the living among the dead? He is not here but has risen! Don't you remember what He told you while He was still in Galilee?"

Then we did remember, but what on earth? Yes, we were still on earth though it didn't really seem like it, what did this mean? Where was Jesus? What were we to understand by this? What were we to do with all the spices and ointments we had prepared? What did "He is risen" really mean? Was it like Lazarus raised from the dead or was it like we would say of the Patriarchs, they died but had gone to Abraham's Bosom and so were living?

Some of our group were so trembling and bewildered. Consternation had so got a grip on them even though the angels had told us to give a specific message to the disciples, as to where Jesus would meet them, they froze, said nothing, and went away.

But I was part of the group that was trying to make sense of it all. We wandered away from the tomb pondering and reasoning, into another part of the beautiful large garden. There was plenty of room to move out of sight of the tomb and it was also near the place of public execution so we could sit on the wall and look down on Golgotha, with the skull so clearly visible in the rock face, in front of which, only three days before we had watched our dearest Friend, and two criminals being crucified.

Here we were in the middle of a mind-blowing situation. What did we really think or believe?

As we looked down at the place of execution with all the people, animals and carts passing by in droves on the main road, we knew that the crosses were empty – each had definitely died, and their bodies were no longer on the crosses. Then we turned our minds to the tomb and knew that the body of Jesus was not there either. Where was His body? Were we really to believe the angels?

Meanwhile, Peter and John had come running to the tomb after Mary had managed to persuade them that Jesus' body was missing. Later, she told us what had happened next. John got there first but stopped outside the tomb. Peter caught him up and went straight in, typical Peter, desperate Peter. There he saw the burial clothes lying on the stone slab where the body had been, but now, there was NO body. Then John went in too and he believed but didn't really understand, so they went back to where they were staying.

But Mary, who had come back with them, was so distraught that she stayed at the tomb, sobbing her heart out. Not only was Jesus dead but now His body had disappeared and she couldn't even minister to Him in His death. As she wept, she stooped down, looked into the tomb, and then she saw the two angels in white sitting there, one at the head and one at the feet where Jesus' body had lain. They said to her, "Woman why are you sobbing?" and she told them, "Because they have taken away My Lord and I don't know where they have laid Him."

With tears streaming down her face and her vision so blurred, she turned around and saw someone outside the tomb who asked her, "Woman, why are you weeping so?" She supposed He was the gardener and replied, "Sir, if you have carried Him from here tell me where you have put Him, and I will take Him away".

Suddenly, as if a bolt of lightning went straight through her whole being, she heard her name called so lovingly, so gently, so deeply by the only person who spoke her name like that and her response was to gasp, "Master," and fall at His feet. There was Jesus, right in front of her, giving her a message for the disciples. Oh her amazement! Oh her joy! Floating on cloud nine, she then went and gave His message to the disciples adding, "I've seen the Lord," but they didn't really believe her.

We knew nothing of what had happened to Mary until we met up with her later. But we had gradually come to terms with what the angels had told us, "He is not here but is risen, go tell His disciples," so we decided to go on our way and deliver the message. As we were about to leave the garden – WOW! - I'll never forget the exquisite, amazing, ginormous shock! Suddenly Jesus met us and said, "Hail." We went straight to Him, clasped His feet and worshipped Him. He told us not to be alarmed or afraid but to tell His disciples to go to Galilee and He'd meet them there, and then He disappeared, just like He apparently had with Mary.

So we went and joined Mary, reinforcing Jesus' message to the disciples, but they really struggled to believe. They were still grieving deeply and were so perplexed, so confused, so frightened and here comes this group of excited women, who of course they knew, telling them that they had seen the Risen Jesus and that they were to go to Galilee, and He'd meet them there.

This was too much for some of them, like Cleopas and his wife Mary. She hadn't been with us in the garden, as she'd possibly stayed with Jesus' mother Mary for she'd been with her at the foot of the Cross on Friday trying to console her. Anyhow they decided it was time to go home to Emmaus, after all, they were exhausted. But I've already told you their story of how Jesus walked with them, giving them the most amazing Bible Study, all about how and why He would suffer, be crucified, and rise from the dead. They suddenly realised Who He was, as He vanished from their sight as they were sitting at the supper table. They were no longer tired, they ran the seven miles back to Jerusalem to where the eleven and the rest of us were gathered together, only to find that Jesus had appeared to Simon Peter.

I never found out how or where that happened because Cleopas and Mary were so excitedly sharing their amazing experience of a seven-mile Bible study, and we were all talking about it and asking questions when suddenly Jesus Himself appeared in the room where we all were, even though the doors were locked because we were afraid of the Jewish leaders. He came and stood among us and said, "Peace to you," and then He showed us His hands, feet and side. At first, many were frightened, startled, and terrified, thinking it was a ghost but as He said, "Peace to you," all the turmoil, horror and anger of the last few days melted away and we were all filled with joy, delight, ecstasy, and rapture, there are not enough words to describe what we all felt. It was epic! It was SO epic!

Here was Jesus literally back from the dead. He was definitely still the Crucified One, He had the scars to prove it, but He was also the Risen One. He walked through solid walls and yet we could touch Him. He was without question our dearest Friend, no one else could do that. He knew that some of the group were still struggling so He asked if they had anything to eat, and they gave Him a piece of broiled fish. He ate it there and then to prove that He still had, if very uniquely, a human body, and was not a ghost.

Then He began to explain to all of us the things that He'd said before His crucifixion and how all that had been written about Him in the Law of Moses, the Prophets and the Psalms, must be fulfilled. He opened our minds so that we really could understand the Scriptures and see that it said that the Christ, The Messiah, would suffer, and then on the third day rise from the dead, and that repentance leading to forgiveness of sins should be preached in His name to all nations beginning in Jerusalem.

Oh! It was so wonderful to begin to understand – this was beyond our wildest imagination, this was far greater than Him coming to free us from the Roman occupation. He explained how all the sacrifices instituted by Moses were each a picture, a shadow, a type, of what He had just done "Once and for All." He had become the final 'At-One-Ment' sacrifice, the final sin offering, the final guilt offering and the final Passover Lamb. We would never need to bring these sacrifices again. The offering of Himself was complete, adequate and totally acceptable to His heavenly Father for all time, and for all people who would choose to accept what He had done for each one of us, and for all who would follow us.

What was so brilliant for us was that Jesus shared all this with us, when most of us women were there. He didn't just share it with the disciples but included all of us. He loved and honoured us all equally.

Chapter 9
A Day or so Later ...

A day or so later those of us who came from Galilee started to return home. Jesus' first message to the disciples had been, "Go to Galilee and I'll meet you there." So off we went, three to four days walking, and so much talking, joy and wondering. It was so good to be out in the open again, not having to lock ourselves in a room to hide from the still very hostile religious leaders in Jerusalem.

You can imagine our conversations, trying to remember everything Jesus had said since His resurrection, but also trying to remember anything and everything He'd said during the last three years. Fortunately, because there were a lot of us, between us we could recall a lot and as we mulled over these things they began to make a lot more sense, as did much of the Scriptures that we'd learnt from childhood. It was amazing, mind-blowing, that 500 years ago, and more, our patriarchs, prophets and poets had said exactly what would happen here in Jerusalem during these last couple of weeks. They had no idea how or when these things would take place, but they so faithfully recorded what the Holy Spirit had said to them, even though they didn't understand.

Our homecoming was so different from what we had expected it to be on Friday or Saturday just past, when our world had been so shattered. Now it had been put back together in a way *far* beyond our wildest dreams. There was still much that we didn't understand but we had JESUS, the Crucified and Risen Jesus – what more could we want?

When we got to our towns and villages and to our homes, we were just bubbling over with our news, and it was hard to remember that life had gone on here just as normal while we'd been away. Not only were we excited about all that had happened in Jerusalem but we were also excited to share with everyone that Jesus was coming to Galilee. We didn't know when, but we guessed it would be fairly soon, meanwhile, we had to wait and get on with everyday life – cooking, cleaning, raising children and grandchildren - all the while keeping in touch for any news of Jesus appearing. It was no use keeping a look out on the Jerusalem to Galilee road because we knew now that Jesus could turn up anywhere, any time. It sure made life exciting and unpredictable!

Peter's wife shared with us how frustrated he got waiting for Jesus to turn up in Galilee, so one night he decided to go fishing again. He hadn't been fishing for a long time, but it was his profession before Jesus called his brother Andrew, their fishing partners, James and John, and himself to join Him and become 'Fishers of Men'. They'd left their father to carry on the business and had been with Jesus for the last three years.

Anyhow, Peter said, "I'm going fishing," and some of the other disciples said, "We'll come with you", so off they went out onto the Sea of Galilee, they knew it so well and they knew how to catch fish but all that night they caught NOTHING. The next morning as day was breaking, Jesus turned up on the beach. They didn't know it was Him but He called out to them, "Guys have you caught any fish?" They had to admit, "No." Then Jesus, a carpenter, told these highly skilled fishermen where to catch the fish, "On the right hand side of the boat," which is the side you don't fish on, so they cast their net on the 'wrong' side of the boat and then couldn't haul it to land, it was such a huge catch of large fish, 153 altogether! John suddenly realised it must be Jesus on the shore who'd given the instructions, and he told Peter, who grabbed his coat and jumped into the sea to get to Jesus as quickly as possible, while the others brought the boat to land where they found fish already cooking on an open fire on the beach and some bread there as well. Jesus invited them to bring some of the fish they'd just caught and have breakfast with Him. I often wondered where Jesus got the fish from.

Peter has an awesome story to tell about what happened straight after breakfast, as Jesus and he went for a walk along the beach, but I'll leave him to tell you about that some other time.

And so it was during the forty days after His resurrection that Jesus appeared to many of us, in different places and on different occasions. One time, He appeared to more than 500 at once, they couldn't all have mistaken someone else for Him, could they? They knew it was Jesus, and He made sure they knew it was Him.

In the next few days, the disciples and most of us women returned to Jerusalem. It was a different journey from the previous one which had ultimately led to His Crucifixion. It had been a strange journey, such a white-knuckle camel ride of emotions. High with the donkey ride into Jerusalem and then, oh my! Rung out to the depths of our beings as we watched Him being crucified and buried. Then, so early on the first day of the week, as we were trying to get a handle on our grief and confusion in the garden where the tomb was, He appeared, right in front of us. Our emotions shot over the moon. Jesus really was alive as the angels had told us, had told US, us WOMEN!

When I think about it, which I do if someone tries to put me down because I'm a woman, I remember it and relive it as a great big gentle hug, an embrace, from Jesus. After all, it IS amazing that He appeared to us women first, before the disciples. But we don't crow about it, He appointed them as apostles and we honour them, but we do enjoy, quietly and deeply, the fact that after His Crucifixion and Resurrection, He still honoured and loved us women in such a special way. No one can take that from us. Not that we are feminists but we enjoy being who God made us to be and knowing that He enjoys us being who He intended us to be. It is such an encouraging comfort even when times are difficult, and they often are.

To be embraced, and hugged, by Almighty God is such an amazing privilege, one that He longs to bestow on each of us so often. One thing I discovered from this was that I no longer needed to try and build up my own self-esteem. He, while on earth, and ever since, esteemed me and that is worth way more than any self-esteem that I can muster, and it also cancels out any low self-esteem that tries to grab me. Who am I to argue with Jesus' opinion of me? Well, I can but it would be pretty stupid to do so. He thought I was worth dying for and that is upliftingly mind-blowing. I hope it is to you too because He also thinks, without any second thought, that you too were worth dying for, that's how much He esteems you and loves you.

Won't you receive His embrace, His hugs, they are like no others. They are wonderfully safe, so healing, so holy, and so heavenly.

Chapter 10
But Here We Are...

Yes, here we are back in Jerusalem and still uncertain as to the future. What is Jesus going to do next? Where is He going to appear next? All we know is that He has told us to wait in Jerusalem for what Father has promised. What has the Father promised? Is He going to restore the kingdom to Israel?

From Resurrection Day for the next forty days, Jesus kept on appearing, and disappearing, and there were many conversations. The disciples asked Him if He was going to re-establish the kingdom and restore it to Israel, but He made it quite clear that the timing was Father's business, and not ours but at the end of forty days, He led us out to the Mount of Olives on the way to Bethany and there He told us so clearly what our business was to be:-

He said, "All authority and power in heaven and on earth has been given to Me, so you are to go and make disciples of all nations, baptising them into the name of the Father and of the Son, and of the Holy Spirit, teaching them to observe everything that I have commanded you, and lo I am with you always and on every occasion to the very close of the age. In My name you will drive out demons, speak in new languages, if you pick up serpents or drink anything deadly it will not hurt you, you will lay hands on the sick and they will be healed. You will receive power when the Holy Spirit has come upon you, and you shall be My witnesses in Jerusalem and all Judea and Samaria and to the ends of the earth."

We were looking at Him, listening intently, trying to take in this amazing Commission He was giving to all of us when all of a sudden, He was caught up in a low-flying cloud that whisked Him away out of our sight into heaven. We were still standing there with our eyes and mouths wide open, when two angels appeared beside us and said, "Men of Galilee, why do you standing gazing into heaven? This same Jesus, who was caught away and lifted up from among you into heaven, will return in just the same way in which you saw Him go into heaven."

WOW!

That was some commissioning service! Jesus made it very clear what He expected us to do, mercifully in *His* power and not our own. We were to preach the Gospel – the Good News – heal the sick, cast out demons, speak in other tongues, raise the dead, disciple nations and be His witnesses, starting in Jerusalem, but going out to the whole world. We didn't even know how big the whole world really was, but we did know that the Roman Empire was pretty large, and this sounded even bigger. We weren't just to disciple ones and twos, but whole nations.

We'd all got used to talking about Jesus to our friends and neighbours, but to whole neighbourhoods, whole towns, whole cities, whole nations, that was a very different matter altogether.

And then, as if that wasn't mind-boggling enough, He was suddenly enveloped in a cloud, that we hadn't seen coming, and which disappeared upwards with Him in it. We were left with two angels, telling us that Jesus would come back in the same way that we'd just seen Him go.

Well, that was comforting and encouraging to know He was coming back. We'd got a little used to His comings and goings during the last forty days, but somehow, we realised this was not quite the same. How could it be when He'd just given us this enormous Commission, even with 120 of us, it certainly couldn't be completed in a fortnight, or even in forty days. Along with Commissioning us to do this, He'd also already told us to wait in Jerusalem and He would send forth upon us, what His Father had promised. We were to, "Wait there until we were clothed with power from on high."

We didn't know what that meant but we did know that we needed to wait in Jerusalem until 'IT' happened. We had no idea how long we would have to wait but we were willing to wait, even in Jerusalem, though it was not the easiest place to be as the opposition from the religious leaders was still very strong.

So, we all went back to the 'upper room', which mercifully was large, and we women, along with the disciples and Mary, Jesus' mother and His brothers, who were now on board completely, spent the time praying together. We did so for ten days. Fifty days after the Passover Sabbath, and ten days after the Ascension, 'IT' happened. We were all praying early in the morning when one of God's 'suddenlies' happened. There was a sound like a rushing violent tempest blast from heaven and it filled the whole house where we were sitting, and then as we looked at one another, wondering if the house would fall in on us, we saw a flame of fire settle on each person there. It didn't hurt us, it didn't burn us, but it filled us right throughout our beings with the Holy Spirit and we began, to our utter amazement, to speak in languages we didn't know at all.

The noise of the wind had been so loud that crowds came running to where we were, and we were so empowered by the Holy Spirit that we spilt out into the streets around and continued speaking in these languages we didn't know only to find that people understood us, even though they came from so many different areas, and even countries, speaking many different dialects and languages.

Some were just bewildered and wondered whatever was happening, while others joked and said we were drunk. But fisherman Peter from Galilee, now so full of the Holy Spirit, stood up with the rest of the disciples, and raising his voice explained exactly what was happening, saying, "These are not drunk as you imagine, after all, it's only nine o'clock in the morning but this is the beginning of what the prophet Joel said would happen, '…that in the last days God said I will pour out My spirit on all people, your sons and daughters will prophesy, your young men will see visions and your old men will dream dreams and on My menservants and My maidservants I will pour out My Spirit and they shall prophesy… and it shall be that whoever calls on the name of the Lord, who adores and worships Him, will be saved."

Then Peter went on to speak so clearly about Jesus and what had happened to Him. He quoted from several of the Psalms and let the people know, without any shadow of a doubt, that they had crucified Jesus, the Lord and Christ, the Messiah. When they heard this, they were cut to their hearts and said urgently to the disciples, "What must we do?" Peter replied, "Repent, change your views and purpose to accept the will of God in your inner selves instead of rejecting it, and be baptised every one of you in the name of Jesus for the forgiveness of your sins and you will receive the gift of the Holy Spirit who is for you and your children."

Peter very seriously spoke a whole lot more to the crowd urging them to be saved from our crooked and perverse generation, with the result that about 3000 people accepted his message, and were baptised that day. My, were we busy that day! These people continued, day after day, to learn from the Apostles, who were teaching in the Temple, and they shared in the Breaking of Bread and in praying together.

As the number of disciples grew at such a phenomenal rate and miracles were happening everywhere in Jerusalem and the Apostles were teaching each day in the Temple and in people's homes, the religious leaders got angrier and angrier; they hated what was happening. When Peter and John, in the name and power of Jesus, healed the lame man who always begged at the Beautiful Gate of the Temple, they arrested them, put them in prison overnight and then ordered them not to speak or teach any more in the name of Jesus. But they replied, "Whether it is right in the sight of God to listen to and obey you rather than God you must decide but we cannot help telling of all we've seen and heard."

Having threatened them, the leaders let them go and they came back to us and we praised and prayed together and asked the Lord to give us full freedom to declare His message faithfully. When we'd prayed, the whole house was shaken and we were all filled again with the Holy Spirit, and we continued to speak the Word of God with freedom, boldness and courage.

There was such amazing, beautiful unity among us. Everyone shared whatever they had, with whoever needed it, and every day more and more people were being saved. More and more miracles were happening. The Apostles would walk down the road and as their shadow fell on the sick people who were lying there, they were instantly healed.

Chapter 11
So, the First Part Was Being Fulfilled

So, the first part of our great Commission from Jesus was being fulfilled. We were witnessing, healing, casting out demons and discipling in Jerusalem, but He had also said in Judea and Samaria, *and* to the ends of the earth. Well, we had to go to Judea, and then Samaria to go home to Galilee. Was Galilee the end of the earth? I think not! So while the Apostles and others continued in Jerusalem fulfilling the Commission there, some of us started to fulfil it further afield. After all, if this needed to be done before Jesus came back, we need to get a move on. We didn't want to delay His return.

It was a much slower journey home than before because we couldn't help but share what we had seen and heard. We were still filled and being filled with the Holy Spirit. We were preaching the Good News, casting out demons, healing the sick, speaking in tongues and making disciples, just as He had told us, and had empowered us to, as we travelled home.

But even now, as you read my story, the Great Commission is only partly fulfilled. It is partly fulfilled because years and years later, you and so many millions have heard our testimony concerning our Crucified, Risen and Ascended Saviour – Jesus, the Messiah. You have believed and been gloriously saved, delivered, healed, baptised and discipled, but the Commission is not complete. There are still millions who haven't heard, believed, been saved, delivered, healed, baptised or been discipled, and because of that Jesus has not yet returned, as the angels said He would when He ascended.

Will you join us, empowered by the Holy Spirit, and share with those around you and those He sends you to the:-

All-powerful,
All-changing
Good news of the Risen and glorified Jesus, the Messiah, Who died and rose again so that everyone might be saved and be part of His Bride that He is coming back for?

His return may be surprisingly soon!

They can't respond if they haven't heard, and they can't hear unless we tell them. What an exciting, amazing Commission is ours – yours and mine – tough yes! But what a privilege!

Will you accept the Commission, maybe for the first time or rededicate yourself to it wherever you are, whatever your nationality, your age, or your circumstances?

There is NO greater calling, and Jesus wants you on board, just as He wanted us, as an active, passionate part of His 'team' because He loves you so much, and those He wants you to share Him with.

Will you come and join us and be Women of the Cross?

First, we ministered to Jesus, He still loves each new generation to do that, and then we obeyed His glorious Commission as soon as we were filled with the Holy Spirit.

What an amazing privilege *was* ours!

What an amazing privilege *is* yours

Dear Women and Men of the Cross!

Meditations for Holy Week

Peter's Dismay

"Could you not watch with Me one brief hour?"

It was a strange Passover meal, unlike the ones we'd previously celebrated with Jesus. He had so much He needed to say to us, we listened but we understood so little of what He was telling us and didn't believe the rest. He told us He was going to die. He told us one of us would betray Him. "Who Lord?"

He told me I would deny Him, deny ever having known Him. "No, Lord! No, Lord! I won't deny You; I'm willing to die for You."

"Before the cock crows twice you will have denied ever having known Me three times." To my utmost shame that is exactly what I did early the next morning.

But before that, after supper, we sang the usual Passover hymns, we were a great male voice choir! Then, after Judas left us when Jesus told him to go and do what he had to do, which was to betray Him to the Chief Priest, though we didn't realise it, the rest of us went with Jesus to the Garden of Gethsemane. Jesus loved to go there to sit among the ancient olive trees and talk to His Heavenly Father. However, this time it was different, it was very dark, and He was distraught.

We were all together and then He called James, John and me to go a little further with Him. He told us to, "Watch and Pray," so that we didn't succumb to temptation and then He went on a little further. He was in great distress, such great distress. We prayed, well we tried to, but we'd had such a good meal, and we'd tried so hard to concentrate on what Jesus was saying, but it was late. To our shame, we lost the battle against sleep.

Oh how awful it was to see the sadness on Jesus' face, indeed on His whole body when He came back and found us asleep. Up until then, we'd always depended on Him and He'd never let us down – now He was depending on us and we immediately let Him down. How awful was that?

But He was so gently gracious asking the question,

"Could you not watch with Me one brief hour?"

Yes, it was gentle, yes, it was gracious, but the question seared through my heart. Couldn't I watch with Him for one brief hour? He was so gracious that He gave us another chance to 'Watch and Pray'.

No one said we had to close our eyes to pray but we just couldn't keep them open, so we failed again and again and by the third time He came back to us, He looked awful. Not only had He been asking His heavenly Father to let Him off what He knew was imminent, death by crucifixion and being cut off from His Father to die carrying all the past, present and future sins of all who ever live on earth. But He was also physically battling to stay alive until He was crucified, the enemy was trying to take Him out before all the prophecies of His death could be fulfilled. Hence when He came back to us, He was sweating great drops of blood, haemorrhaging through His skin, but He held it all together. He had told Father that He would go through with the plan. Then He called us all together saying, "The time has come, the betrayer is at hand."

At that moment, Judas appeared in the garden with a whole band of men with swords and clubs from the Chief Priests and rulers. He had told them that the person He greeted with a kiss was the person they were to arrest, and he came straight to Jesus and kissed Him.

So, it was Judas. How could he betray Jesus who'd loved him, cared for him, and trusted him for three years, just like He had the rest of us? How could he do it? How could he do it? Anger was welling up inside me. Anger at myself for having failed three times to do what Jesus had asked me to do, to 'Watch and Pray' and I couldn't even manage an hour. How pathetic was that? Tough guy Peter, who was used to being up all night fishing, and I couldn't even stay awake to stand by my best friend for an hour when He especially needed me. In addition to that, there was my anger against Judas.

How? How? How could he do this? How could he bring this rabble into the garden and intrude so relentlessly on Jesus' need for quiet and solitude at this time? Couldn't he see Jesus was in great distress? No, he couldn't and that too made me angry. I was so angry! Never before had I used a sword, but I had one and I used it in my anger, but also in defence of Jesus. I had to prove that I loved Him in spite of letting Him down. I used it and sliced Malchus' ear right off. How I only sliced off his ear I'll never know, that was the mercy of God. I was very pleased that I'd done it, he deserved it, they all deserved it. But Jesus' reaction just took the stuffing out of me because in the middle of all the noise, chaos and anger, He just miraculously put Malchus' ear back, completely healed. You would have thought that would have stopped the crowd, but it didn't. But it certainly diminished the grandeur of my heroic gesture, it had been pointless except that it had vented some of my anger and it showed me that retaliation is not God's way.

Jesus, in His love, insisted that He was the person they had come for and no one else, so we got out of the way, but I followed at a distance. It was my undoing. I ended up sitting round the enemy's fire while the Chief Priests and others, were mocking Jesus and making trumped-up charges against Him. Yes, it was a cold night, and I was cold through and through, but I wanted to know what was happening to my dearest friend. This was the nearest I could get – round the enemy's fire – but it was such a dangerous place to be. I was so vulnerable, so much more vulnerable than I realised. So tired, so cold, so traumatised and to my very, very great shame before the cock crowed twice, I denied ever having known Jesus three times. Oh, how could I have done that? How could I have possibly done that?

I was sitting with the wrong people around the wrong fire, very easy to do, but very dangerous. I'm so grateful that Jesus knew my heart better than I knew it myself, and after the Resurrection, He invited me to His fire on the beach in Galilee where He had prepared breakfast for us and He made it so clear that He had forgiven me.

I can't thank Him enough for His forgiveness and for paying the enormous cost of taking my sins on Himself, on the Cross so that I could be forgiven.

Had I 'Watched and Prayed for one brief hour', my story might have been very different and had I not sat around the enemy's fire and tried to blend in, I wouldn't have known the shame of denying Him the way I did.

Are there times when, like me, you leave yourself vulnerable to the enemy's tactics?

Are there times when the Holy Spirit prompts you to pray but you're too tired or too busy?

Are there times when you sit around the wrong fire, just to enjoy the warmth of the company or not wanting to stand out from the 'others'?

Yes, Jesus forgave me, but it still grieves me that I let Him down so easily.
Thankfully it wasn't the end of my relationship with Him, but after His Resurrection, His unmerited forgiveness spurred me on to give my life totally to Him, no matter what the cost. And it did cost, but He was and is so worth it.

Pilate's Dilemma
John 18:28-40

Oh, the Dilemma!

It was early in the morning, and suddenly there was a noisy, determined crowd at the door.

Shall I make them wait or shall I invite them in?

I invited them in, but they wouldn't come. My palace wasn't clean enough for them!

Shall I go out to them or let them stew in their own taboos?

Does it matter if they are fit to eat the Passover later tonight or not? What's in a meal?

I went out to them. Why had they come? What was the urgency?

How should I handle this volatile situation? Yes, it was a dilemma and it seemed to be getting more intense by the minute.

"What accusations do you bring against this man?"

This man, Jesus, I'd heard so much good about, this man who'd healed the sick, fed the hungry and even raised the dead. Yes, I'd heard about Him and I liked what I'd heard. He was no threat to Caesar's throne, after all, He only rode into the city the other day on a DONKEY, and the people got happily excited. He didn't come in on a white charger as a conquering hero trying to overthrow Rome.

"What is your accusation?" I asked. "He's an evildoer," they replied.

"Well take Him yourselves, judge, sentence and punish Him according to your own laws." Surely this was the way out of the dilemma?

But NO, they wanted Him killed but they didn't have the authority to authorise that, BUT they were determined.

What to do?

I retreated into the Judgement Hall with all the confidence and dignity I could muster.

I called Jesus to stand before me.

I wanted justice for Jesus, but I needed to save my own skin as well.

Was it possible to do both?

"Are you the King of the Jews?"

He didn't answer my question instead He asked me if that was my opinion or just what others had told me. That was a challenge and increased my dilemma.

So I asked a different question, "What have you done that has caused your own leaders to bring you here?" But again, He didn't answer my question.

He started talking about His 'Kingdom' and I suppose began to answer my first question, "Was He the King of the Jews?" He said, "My kingdom is not of this world." So, He has a Kingdom so He must be a King, but His Kingdom is not of this world? "How can that be?"

He explained that if it had been, His followers would have been fighting on His behalf to keep Him safe from the Jewish leaders, but they weren't because His Kingdom was not of this world. Then what world does His Kingdom belong to?

I didn't understand so I asked Him again, "Are you a King?" He answered that I was right, He was a King, but His Kingdom was the Kingdom of Truth. Did He mean that it was a philosophical kingdom? Truth was a pretty scarce commodity around here, either amongst the Romans, the Jews, the Greeks or anyone else, they all had their own idea of what was Truth depending on what suited them, it was all relative.

I asked Jesus, "What is Truth?" I didn't wait for an answer because here I saw the way out of my dilemma. I could tell the Jewish leaders and the crowd there was no problem. I could find no fault in Him because all He was claiming was a philosophical kingdom, not a physical one, so neither they nor Rome needed to be worried.

So, I offered to release Jesus as it was Passover - it was customary for me to release one prisoner each year at this time. But they were adamant, yelling not to release Jesus, but Barabbas, who was an awful guy. Oh, the dilemma...and it increased, what else could I do? How could I give Jesus justice and save my own skin? I'll appease the anger by having Him flogged, scourged, and whipped, surely that would be enough. They'd think I was on their side really even though I wasn't, but it would get them off my back wouldn't it?

I had to compromise somehow. Surely that was acceptable in these circumstances?

The soldiers went way beyond what I asked but that made it look better for me. They made a crown of thorns and rammed it on Jesus' head, they threw a purple cloak around Him having stripped Him to beat Him, they mocked Him and they slapped Him.

So, I went out to the people again, surely, they would be satisfied now? I took a stand, I told them I found NO fault in Him but as soon as they saw Him, they were baying for Him to be crucified.

Again, I said, "I find NO fault in Him." Yes, I took my stand momentarily, but I was terrified because they cited the law against blasphemy, which says that the punishment for claiming to be God was death.

Oh, it was getting worse and worse and all I'd tried to do was placate, to bring peace, to calm the situation, but I was rapidly discovering that compromise and this sort of diplomacy didn't work. And then it started affecting my family, even my wife had a really bad dream. She sent a message to the Judgement Hall warning me to, "Have nothing to do with this just and upright man." It was a bit late for that warning, I was up to my neck in it.

I asked Jesus again "Where are you from?" but He didn't answer. I explained that I had the power and the authority to release Him or crucify Him, so He'd better answer me. To which He replied, "You would not have any authority whatsoever over Me if it was not given you from above." Wow! I had thought I had a lot of authority from Rome but as the hours passed I realised I had a lot less authority than I thought, and then Jesus stood in front of me, telling me to my face that I actually had no authority except what was being given to me from 'above'. It didn't seem to be very much but I did try as hard as I could to release Him. He knew that and strangely, comforted me, by telling me that Judas' sin was greater than mine!

But the crowd kept yelling and reminding me that if I let Jesus, who said He was the King of the Jews go, I would no longer be Caesar's friend.

They would see to it, and that would be my head literally on the block. I capitulated, though I kept on reminding them that He was their King and handed Him over to be crucified. But on the plaque that was fastened to His cross, I wrote, "Jesus the Nazarene, King of the Jews."

They wanted me to change it but I refused. I did believe He was the King of the Jews and wrote it in Hebrew, Latin and Greek so that all who passed by could read it. The 1st letters of each word on the sign in Aramaic (Hebrew) were Y-H-W-H, which was the Hebrew way of writing the sacred name Yahweh.* No wonder the Chief Priests were offended, but I insisted.

I was devastated, desperate, and horrified, reliving all these hours.

How could I have done things differently? Had I really authorised the death of the King of the Jews? Or the King of somewhere else, come to that? How was I ever going to live with all this for the rest of my life?

I was in turmoil. I longed to get off the planet. I wanted the ground to swallow me up. I'd been shown up for the weakling that I was. I would never have the people's respect again, if I'd ever had it, and I had certainly lost all my self-respect. I'd learned a big lesson, that justice and compromise do not go together, it's one or the other.

What was I to do?

Suddenly my frenetic thinking was interrupted by one of my minions.

"No! I don't want to be disturbed, I'm disturbed enough already"

"But Sir, it's one of the Pharisees'

"I've seen enough of that angry mob"

'No, this one isn't angry, he's trembling, he's fearful"

"OK, let him in"

I tried to pull my shattered dignity together. Whatever did he want?

He was ashen. He was indeed fearful. Whatever did he want? I was amazed, he wanted my permission to take the body of Jesus, Who, surprisingly was already dead, before the soldiers threw Him into a common grave. Why?

It turned out that like me, Joseph of Arimathea believed that Jesus was the King of the Jews. Indeed, he had become a secret disciple of His but, like me, he hadn't been able to stand up against the rest of the Jewish council, even though he so wanted to. But now, he had the courage to take a stand and let it be known that he believed that Jesus was their Messiah.

His heartbreak, his grief, and turmoil were as real, and as raw as mine. I wasn't supposed to let him know how I felt. I willingly gave my permission for him to take the body and bury it with all the tender grace and dignity that he could muster in his anguish.

He was fortunate, at least there was something practical he could do to show how sorry he was that he'd been such a coward. But what could I do to show how sorry I was? It was indeed a dilemma, such a terrible dilemma. Had Jesus realised how many times I'd tried to stand up for Him? How many times I said 'I find no fault, no crime in Him.' Oh, I do hope so.

Oh no! Not that angry mob again. What do they want now? Haven't they got all they wanted? Jesus was crucified, certified dead by one of my centurions and buried. They were clamouring at my palace door again, but their mood had changed from anger, outright blatant anger, to irrational agitation. Why? They remembered that He had said to them, "After three days I will rise again," and strangely, having just had Him killed, they obviously believed that this might happen otherwise it wouldn't have worried them. Although they did try to make out that Jesus' disciples might make His resurrection appear to have happened by stealing the body away. They were demanding that I give an order for the tomb to be sealed and made secure, with a continuous guard of soldiers watching it.

I told them to take a guard of their own soldiers and make the tomb as safe and secure as they possibly could, it was up to them to do that. Off they went to see to it and I was left to ponder. Was there any chance that Jesus, the King of the Jews, as I really believed Him to be, could actually resurrect Himself after being dead for three days? Yes, I knew that Jesus had brought Jairus' daughter back to life, but was she really dead at the time? After all, she was still at home. But then there was the widow of Nain's son. He was in the coffin on his way to be buried when Jesus interrupted the funeral and gave him back to his mother alive. Oh yes, 1 knew what was going on in my 'patch', I had my spies!

Then there was Lazarus, he'd definitely been dead four days when Jesus called him out of the tomb in Bethany. Was it possible that He could raise Himself from the dead? It would prove that He was even more, so much more than the King of the Jews, His kingdom must surely then be of another world, as He told me, if He did rise from the dead.

Oh, I longed that He would indeed rise from the dead, but my reasoning said it was not possible, it was completely NOT possible, but if He did? If He did and if I could meet Him again, I would fall at His feet and ask His forgiveness for putting my life before His, after all, He is the King of the Jews and so much more, and I'm only a puppet of Rome. His integrity was such that I do believe He would forgive me. What a man! What a king! This is who Israel needs! This is who each one of us needs.

What are your dilemmas? Maybe they are not as awful as mine, maybe they are worse. Will you let Him deal with all your dilemmas?

I believe He is the only One who can really meet us in our dilemmas and clearly direct us through them, day by day.

Proverbs 3: 5-7 says, "Lean on, trust and be confident in the Lord with all your heart and mind and do not rely on your own insight or understanding. In all your ways know Him, and He will direct and make straight and plain your paths. Be not wise in your own eyes; reverently fear and worship the Lord and turn entirely away from evil."

He loves to deal with our dilemmas if we will invite Him to do so.

* See footnote to John19:19-20 (TPT)

The Desperate Journey From the Cross to the Tomb

It was not very far from the Cross to the Tomb, but it was no quick and easy journey in the dark for Joseph of Arimathea and Nicodemus, two highly respected members of the Jewish council.

The journey began so publicly. They had to ask Pilate for the body of Jesus, and then back at the Cross, they would have been seen by Jews and Romans alike. taking responsibility for the burial of the body. There was no more hiding, their reputations were gone, shattered.

While Jesus was alive, they remained secret disciples, now that He was dead, and as far as they knew not coming back to life, they found the courage, humility and brokenness to take, whatever care they could, of this One whom they had come to respect, know and believe in. They were willing to lose their reputation for Jesus, even for a DEAD Jesus.

Are we? Am I?

They were extravagant in their caring. It was probably the tomb Joseph had prepared for himself that they laid Jesus in. Nicodemus brought 75 pounds of myrrh, aloes and linen to wrap the lacerated, pierced, torn, bloodied, unrecognisable body of Jesus in.

What extravagance!

They were willing to be completely associated with Jesus' brokenness, indeed to be contaminated by it. They couldn't anoint and wrap a dead body without touching it, nor could they carry it without being touched by it, it couldn't even be carried at arm's length. They would have to embrace the body. Would they have slung the body of Jesus over their shoulders and marched from the Cross to the Tomb? Or would they have taken all the care they could, to carry the battered body as gently as possible, even though it was a dead body?

To carry Him gently they would have to hold Him, literally close to their hearts, and identify with Him. As they carried Him, their hearts and minds, which must have already broken during the previous 24 hours must have been shattered. But they were willing to carry the crucified Jesus in public and in private.

Imagine the journey from the Cross to the Tomb, not very far, but taken with every effort not to inflict more pain on the wrecked body, even though it was dead. Taking such care where they walked, so as not to stumble on the way. There was no worn path from the Cross to the Tomb, and it was a dark journey.

Are we willing to walk with them and learn how to carry the crucified body of Jesus, as well as the Resurrected one? He is still the crucified one.

As they journeyed, what happened when they saw people who knew them and didn't approve of what they were doing? Did they drop the body of Jesus on the ground, and stand in front of it, hoping their long robes would hide Him and their embarrassment? How would that help? Their robes would have betrayed them, for they must have been covered with the blood of Jesus and perfumed with the myrrh and aloes.

But oh, the privilege of carrying the Saviour of the world, their Messiah from the Cross to the Tomb, of ministering to Him in His darkest hours, expecting to get nothing in return, except ridicule from the people, and disgust from all the other spiritual leaders.

How do we, you and I, carry the Crucified One? He still is the Crucified One and He always will be, even though He is also the Risen One. Will we hold Him, close to our hearts, and publicly, and with such love and gentle care, will we carry Him daily from the Cross to the Tomb?

When we take the bread and the wine, His Body and His Blood, into our bodies in love, in gratitude, in humility, in brokenness and obedience to His Word, we are holding Him so close to our hearts. It is there where He, and our heavenly Father, and the Holy Spirit love to be, carried very carefully and with immense love in our hearts continuously day by day.

The Divine Invitation

'Daddy, Abba, is it time to sit up at the table?'

"Yes, My child, leave your toys, leave your troubles and come and sit next to My Son."

'Daddy, Abba, what is for supper?'

"It's the same as usual, bread and wine, but it's always fresh, always vintage, delicious and sustaining."

'Daddy, Abba, how much may I eat?'

"You may have as much as you can eat, drink and digest."

'But Daddy will there always be enough?'

"Yes, My dear child there will always be enough for you and everyone else who comes to share in My Son's banquet. It's like when He fed the 5000 plus, there was plenty left over, plenty left for others. At His banquet there will always be, even though millions come, there will always be enough. It will always be fresh, and it will always re-fill and re-energize you, if you take time to sit down with Him and don't think it's a take-away you can grab as you rush through your day."

'Daddy, Abba, will there be waiters and waitresses like at a proper banquet?'

"No, My child there won't be, because this is a very intimate banquet and My Son Himself will serve each one of you who comes and takes time to sit with Him."

'Daddy, Abba, what shall I wear to the banquet? My clothes are not very clean, and I've got grazes on my knees, what shall I do?'

"Tell Me how your clothes got dirty, and how your knees got grazed."

'Well, it was like this Daddy, I ...... I....... I....... and I..... I'm so sorry, please, will You forgive me?'

"Thank you, My Child, because you have been honest with Me I'm glad to forgive you. My Son has already taken the punishment for all the things you've done, the things you've left undone, the things that you've said, the things you've left unsaid and the things you've thought which have made Me so sad. Because you have asked for My forgiveness and really don't want to do these things again, I have a banqueting robe made specially for you. When you put it on it will hide your dirty clothes and they will become spotlessly clean, and your grazed knees will be healed very quickly."

'Daddy, Abba, can I see my new robe?'

"Yes, My child, here it is."

'Oh, Daddy it's so beautiful, it's so pure. It's just like Your Son's.'

"Yes, My Son took some of His robe to make yours."

'Can I put it on?'

"Yes."

'Oh! it's wonderful! Does it suit me?'

"Yes, indeed it does. You look fantastic to Me."

"Come My child, whatever your age, sit right close to My Son and hear His heart for you, and for My children all around the world. Come and sit at His table, clothed in your robe of rightness and My Son will feed you with His Bread and Wine, with His Body and Blood, with His life.

If you listen carefully, expectantly and excitedly, He will share some of Our precious secrets with you. You can then share, not only in the banquet but in other things that We are doing and are longing to do around the world."

"Come to Our table and enjoy Our passion, enjoy Our presence and enjoy Our provision."

'Oh Daddy, Abba, and Jesus I'm coming, and I'm so excited.'

'Thank you so much for making it possible for me to come to Your banquet. Thank you that You will never, ever turn me away. I'm SO grateful.'

"Come often as a child, whatever your age."

GIVEN

"Take it and eat your fill.
It is My body which is *given* for you.
Do this to remember Me."

1 Corinthians 11 v 24

Jesus says, "Eat your fill" that equals "eat and be satisfied". It's not a one-off meal. It's a meal to be repeated so that we remember, and remember, and remember, what He has done for us.

He said, "This is My body GIVEN for you."

We are 'fore-given' because our horrendous debt has already been paid in advance. God is SO generous, He GIVES and GIVES and GIVES.

John 14:27 (KJV) – "Peace I leave with you. My peace I GIVE unto you, not as the world giveth give I unto you. Let not your heart be troubled nor let it be afraid."

John 15:11 (NLT) – "I have told you these things so that you will be filled with My joy. Yes, your joy will overflow."

Matthew 11:28 (KJV) – "Come unto Me all you who are weary and heavy laden (overburdened) and I will GIVE you rest."

Ezekiel 36:26 (KJV) – "I will GIVE you a new heart and a new spirit I will put within you. I will remove from you your heart of stone and GIVE you a heart of flesh."

Psalm 2:8 (NTL) – "Only ask and I will GIVE you the nations as your inheritance, the whole earth as your possession."

Isaiah 62:2 (NET Bible) – "You will be called by a new name that the Lord Himself will GIVE you."

When we ask for for-giveness we are drawing on a cheque that has already been paid in full, and the account will never get overdrawn.

Isaiah 50:5-6 – "I did not resist. I did not rebel. I offered (gave) My back to those who flogged Me and My cheek to those who tore out My beard."

1 Peter 2:24 – "He Himself carried our sins in His body on the cross so that we would be dead to sin and live for righteousness. Our instant healing flowed from His wounding."

Isaiah 53:5 (NLT) – "He was pierced for our rebellion, crushed for our sins. He was beaten so we could be whole. He was whipped so we could be healed."

Fore-given =
Given in advance

Do we fore-give or are we, am I reticent to exonerate? (Exonerate – to free, from guilt and blame)
"Dear Jesus You gave, have given, offered Your body for me and You tell me to 'Eat my fill', to eat and be satisfied. You are always more than enough to fill me, to satisfy all my cravings. I know that in my mind and in theory, but how do I eat and be continually satisfied?
Lord, Proverbs 9:3 says, 'The Lord satisfies the longings of His lovers'
So, what am I to conclude?'
Is it that I'm not truly one of Your lovers?
Or am I spiritually anorexic?
Or am I spiritually lazy?
Or am I spiritually blind to what You set before me to eat daily?
Or am I unwilling to pick up a knife and fork to eat the meat You give, and only pick up a straw to drink milk?
Or am I so hungry that I only get temporary satisfaction and then want more?

Oh, please teach me how to feast on You, Who gave Yourself, in order that I might be satisfied daily. Oh, thank You, dear Jesus."

Our God is SO generous. He GAVE His amazingly perfect self that we might be 'fore-given'. He 'FORE-GAVE' us when He was on the Cross for all we have done and will do. "Father, 'FORE-GIVE' them they don't know what they are doing."

What should our response be? Surely to receive this amazing gift for ourselves on a daily basis, and then, GIVE it to any who have hurt or offended us whether they ask for it or not.

Jesus 'fore-gave' us when He was on the Cross, He didn't wait till we asked to be forgiven. What a wonderful, gracious 'fore-giving' saviour we have!

"Oh, thank You Lord, may I continuously eat and remember what You have done, even for me. May I never forget or belittle the enormity of your personal 'fore-giveness' for me."

He Shed His Life-Giving Blood

"At the end of the last Passover meal that Jesus had with His disciples, having explained to them about the bread being His body, He then took the last cup of wine in His hands and said, 'This cup seals the New Covenant with My blood. Drink it, and whenever you drink it, do it in remembrance of Me.'"

1 Corinthians 11: 25

Jesus' New Covenant fulfilled the Old Covenant once and for all. Under the Old Covenant, the people who wanted to be right with God had to offer specific sacrifices every year to show that they were truly sorry for the sins they had committed during that year. Each year a perfect lamb was killed in their place. The blood of the lamb was poured out.

Jesus is saying to His disciples, then and now, I am making the complete, efficacious, everlasting, one-off sacrifice, which is sufficient for all who choose to believe in Me, are truly sorry for their sin, really repent, turn their back on their sin, and follow Me. Jesus' blood is completely sufficient, there is nothing that we can add to it, and there is no sin that it doesn't cover or include.

Blood poured from His head as the crown of thorns was rammed into His head. His shed blood can cover all the sinful thoughts we have ever thought if we confess them, and truly repent.

Blood poured from His hands and wrists as they nailed Him to the Cross. His shed blood can cover all the sinful things we have ever done, and all the good things we have ever left undone if we confess them, and truly repent.

Blood poured from His feet as they nailed Him to the Cross. His shed blood can cover all the sinful places we have ever been to, and the good places that we haven't been to that He wanted us to go to if we confess them, and truly repent.

Blood poured from His side, His heart, as He was pierced by the soldier's sword. His shed blood can cover all our sinful emotions and feelings if we confess them, and truly repent.

But not only does His blood *cover* all the sins that we really acknowledge, but it also *cleanses* us from them to the extent that in Hebrews 8:12 God says, "For I will be merciful and gracious towards their wickedness, and I will remember their sins **no more**."

The blood that Jesus shed is able to wipe our slate absolutely clean if we bring it to Him, acknowledge what is on it, and ask Him to apply His precious blood. Mercifully, the supply of Jesus' shed blood will never come to an end, while there are sinners on the earth who need it applied to their, and our lives.

This is the New Covenant that He has made with us, "If we freely admit our sins when His light uncovers them, He *will* be faithful to forgive us every time. God *is* just to forgive us our sins because of Christ and He *will* continue to cleanse us from all unrighteousness" - 1 John 1:9

So, as we drink the fruit of the vine, as He has asked us to do, let us marvel afresh and remember each time that:

1) He has made the most amazing covenant with us, that He cannot break, and has sealed it with His Blood.
2) He has covered all the sins that we have acknowledged and repented of with His Blood.
3) He has wiped our slate completely clean with His Blood.

And to do all that He really had to die in your place and mine.

How amazing is that?
'Oh, thank you, Jesus'.

A Ponder Page

This page is for you and God only, so fill it in honestly. Take it with you and re-read it as often as you need to. Use as much additional paper as you need to.

1) How eager am I to come to the 'Lord's Table'?
Why is that?

Why do I come?

2) How do I react to the thought that Jesus is serving me with His own Body and Blood?

3) Before I partake do I always tell Him truthfully how my 'clothes got dirty and my knees got grazed,' and ask His forgiveness? 1 Corinthians 11:27-32

4) Do I really believe God has a robe of 'right-ness' tailor-made for me? (Not one that fits my ideas but His).
If so – Why?

If not – Why?

5) Do I treat Communion like a 'takeaway' to grab as I rush through the day, or as a time to come and 'be' in God's presence?

6) Do I come full of what I want to tell Him, or do I come quietly to listen expectantly to what He wants to whisper to me?

7) Do I believe that He wants to share precious secrets with me?

8) Do I really believe that the dear Trinity, Father, Jesus and Holy Spirit, really want me to come to Their table and enjoy Their Presence, enjoy Their Passion and enjoy Their Provision?

If not –Why not?

9) Do I consider Communion a poverty meal or an amazing banquet?

Why?

Jesus' Dearest Desire, How Long?

"My dear friends I am so glad you have spent time with Me this week, but how long will you enjoy my Resurrection?

How long will you enjoy meeting Me, your risen Lord, at the empty tomb, in the upper room, or by the Sea of Galilee?

How long will your heart burn within you as it did for those two on the road to Emmaus, when I joined them in their loneliness, their grief and their sadness?

I long for you to be a Resurrection people not just this weekend, but every weekend. Not just this week, but every week. Not just this month, or this year, but every month and year, until I bring you home to the complete, amazing Resurrection Celebration.

There is only one way for you to be a continuous Resurrection people, a spontaneous Resurrection person, and that way is to spend time with Me.

Spend time with Me at the Last Supper, be My special guest at this unhurried meal.

Watch and Listen and Hear My Heart.

Spend time with Me in the Garden of Gethsemane, come and share My anguish, My heartache, My heartbreak. Come and share My loneliness, My fear of What was to come any minute. My battle to do Father's will whatever the cost even though I could have opted out.

Come, Watch and Listen, Hear My Heart.

Spend time with Me as they led Me away and falsely accused Me, mocked Me, and tortured Me, so unjustly and to such extremes.

Come, Watch and Listen, Hear My Heart.

Spend time with Me as My friend betrayed Me, as another denied ever having known Me, as the others ran away.

Come, Watch and Listen, Hear My Heart.

Come, walk with Me to Golgotha as I stagger under the weight of the Cross on my broken body and My broken heart.

Come, Watch and Listen, Hear My Heart.

Will you stand at the foot of the Cross with Mary and John? Will you dare to hold My nail-pierced feet, and wash them with your tears in spite of all the mocking and jeering going on around?

Will you watch and listen and hear My heart during those three terrible hours of darkness? Will you spend time with Joseph of Arimathea and Nicodemus, as they go and face Pilate and then carry My body to the tomb and so lavishly pour out their love?

Come, Watch and Listen, Hear My Heart.

Will you spend time with the dear women who came so early to the tomb on Sunday morning? What was their Saturday like?

Oh, please, Watch and Listen and Hear My Heart.

If you will do this often, not just once a year, but often, then I promise you I will meet with you at the empty tomb, and your mind will be blown as I call you by name.

I will walk the road to your Emmaus with you as many times as you walk it, and your heart will burn within you as I open up the Scriptures to you.

I will meet you by the Sea of Galilee – I will have a meal ready for you and you will know that I have forgiven you, and I will give you direction and responsibilities.

As you continue to spend time with Me – Watching, Listening and Hearing My Heart, you will understand in your heart, as well as, your mind more and more how much I love you personally. More and more, you will receive My passion for you, and the more you will live as Resurrection People.

As you watch and listen and hear My heart you may ask Me questions, but primarily watch so carefully, listen so attentively so that you hear My very heartbeat, for you and the world. Then you will live 24/7 as Resurrection people and the whole of Heaven will stand, applaud and ring with Hallelujahs, crying, "Worthy is the Lamb who was slain, to receive power and wealth and wisdom and might and honour and glory and blessing" – Revelation 5:12.

As you come and take the Bread and the Wine, invite My Holy Spirit to enable you to become more deeply, than ever before, a Resurrection person. You cannot do it by yourself, but He is longing to enable you for this because…

I AM SO PASSIONATE

ABOUT YOU!'

The Passion of The Christ
Christ's Passionate Passion

"Oh, the passion! the passion!

I have such a passion.

I have such a passion for my people.

They are all My people, you are all My people.

I created each one. I love them. I love you so dearly.

I created them, I created you so clearly, so individually, so specially. Like the snowflakes, every person I created is different, is unique, is beautiful, but for each person, their beauty has been hidden from birth, that's why I came and loved so passionately.

That's why I came to die - to release each one from all that cloaks their beauty.

Whatever you need to clean, whatever is cloaked or choked with dirt, you must use the right cleaning agent, whether it's cleaning the silver, the chimney, or the blocked drain.

To restore them to how they should be you have to use the right thing and there is only ONE right thing that will clean a person, and remove all that cloaks their beauty and usefulness and that is My Blood – that's why I came to die, why I'm so passionate about all My people.

I designed each person beautiful but each has a hideous cloak, even the best of which is awful in My eyes. Yet, I'm so passionate about you that I came to shed My Blood for you, personally, so that your sin could be done away with, that you could be spotless and sparklingly clean inside and out and receive new life from Me.

"I came that you may have Life and have it more abundantly."

– John 10:10.

What are *you* passionate about?

Is it about making the best you can out of life?

Is it about improving your situation?

Is it about helping your neighbour?

Or dare I hope that, just as I am so passionate about you, you would become more and more passionate about Me so that I can share My heart with you and together, you and I, we can be really passionate about what matters most in My heart.

Will you acknowledge your sin and your need to be rid of it by bringing it to the foot of the Cross and exchanging it for the *Bread and the Wine*?

There is nothing magical about this bread and wine but if you leave your sin here, and eat and drink in faith, My sacrifice will clean you on the inside first and then gradually, My beauty will be seen by others in you and radiate out from you.

This is My passion, and oh! - it's all for you.

    You may take it or leave it,

        But I have given it,

            Given it,

                Given Myself freely *for* you and *to* you.

Calvary - the Cross is My passionate love for you."

About the Author

As a teenager Fran kept failing her school exams and her report frequently said 'she has no imagination', but as an adult she loved teaching Physical Education to secondary school youngsters making sure everyone enjoyed it no matter what their ability or lack of it.

She also enjoyed sharing the Bible with the girls in school and in the national Christian youth work she was involved with for many years. She also led Bible study groups in Church.

After 11 years of teaching God called her to leave and totally unexpectedly she landed up volunteering in her friend, Judith's, tiny wool shop where the Holy Spirit gave her stunning designs to create bespoke knitted garments having had NO previous knitting experience and 'no imagination' – But God! Within the shop they opened up a section selling Christian books and led a weekly Bible Study group for customers who wanted to join them. After another 11 years God called time on that venture and 3 years later gave Fran the blueprint for a Christian centre that He wanted to establish and in 1990 along with Judith, who by then was 78, and other volunteers she began the conversion of a derelict 4 story building into a 42 bedded Christian retreat centre which is still running having survived two major floods and a very major fire.

During the later years there, they had Holy Week Meditations with Scripture readings, reflective worship, led beautifully by Ann, followed by a meditation which Fran wrote and which now form the second part of this book with the prayer that you will be as blessed by them as the folk who first heard them. Having retired and moved away from the Centre after 27 years Fran now has more time to wait on God and this book is part of what He has graciously downloaded to her. Yes, she has retired, but God has kindly re-tyred her for the next part of her journey – volunteering at the amazing Harbour Centre in Bedworth, run by Life Church. What a huge privilege to walk alongside so many heart-achingly needy people and share the love of Jesus with them in many different ways.`

www.ingramcontent.com/pod-product-compliance
Lightning Source LLC
Chambersburg PA
CBHW060504080526
44584CB00015B/1535